DEC 0 0 2020

# Seeking the Spiritual Path

*A Collection*

*from Lifeline*

ISBN: 978-1-889681-06-1

Library of Congress Control No.: 2007929614

Overeaters Anonymous, Inc.

World Service Office

6075 Zenith Court NE

Rio Rancho, New Mexico 87144-6424 USA

Mailing address: PO Box 44020

Rio Rancho, NM 87174-4020 USA

505-891-2664

www.oa.org

# PREFACE

Compulsive overeating is a threefold disease, and the foundation of Overeaters Anonymous is threefold recovery: physical, emotional, and spiritual. This book is a collection of stories and commentaries about spiritual recovery.

Written by OA members for OA members, these stories first appeared in *Lifeline*, OA's magazine of recovery. The opinions expressed are those of the individual authors and do not represent OA as a whole. Their words are not intended to give definitive answers to personal questions about spirituality; rather, they reflect many different experiences of spiritual discovery and growth.

Wherever you are in your spiritual recovery, may you find encouragement in these pages.

# TABLE OF CONTENTS

## Preface

## CHAPTER ONE:
### The Search for a Higher Power

*These OA members were pleasantly surprised to learn that they could welcome a Higher Power of their understanding into their lives.*

# CHAPTER TWO:
## Turning Our Lives and Our Will Over to a Higher Power

*It isn't easy to hand control over to HP, but these OA members found that the program would work only if they did so.*

## CHAPTER THREE:
### A Spiritual Solution to Our Disease

*Developing a relationship with the Higher Power of our understanding and working the Twelve Steps pave the road to freedom from compulsive eating.*

## CHAPTER FOUR:
### Spiritual Experiences Before and During the Program

*God brought these individuals to OA—and kept them there.*

## CHAPTER FIVE:
### Connecting with Higher Power

*Prayer and meditation yield gratitude and serenity, the gifts of the program.*

## CHAPTER SIX:
### By the Grace of God

*Higher Power's love and acceptance brought profound changes to the lives of these OA members.*

## CHAPTER SEVEN:
### Agnostics and Atheists: A Unique Perspective

*Some OA members found the spiritual principles of the program challenging—and surprisingly uplifting.*

## CHAPTER EIGHT:
### Tools for Spiritual Growth

*These OA members use the Steps, the tools, and literature to grow spiritually.*

# CHAPTER ONE

# The Search for a Higher Power

*These OA members were pleasantly surprised to learn that they could welcome a Higher Power of their understanding into their lives.*

# Spiritual Awakening

I've often heard people talk about trudging through the Steps, and how they wish they could have a "burning bush" type of spiritual experience, rather than the slow, educational type that most OA members get by working the Steps—as if this would vault them into happiness, joy, and freedom forever.

I had such an experience several years ago, when I was locked up in a treatment center and forced to do Fourth and Fifth Steps to gain my freedom. I had completed my Fifth Step. The minister hearing it asked me if I wished to pray with him, and I said I would, although I thought it was pretty ridiculous and silently hoped no one would come into the room and see us.

> *I forgive you before you ever do the things you need forgiveness for.*

The moment he knelt and took my hand, my God rushed into the room. I won't attempt to explain this—what it felt like to be in the same room with God's presence surrounding me, because that would be impossible. As the minister began praying, I could hear his words clearly, yet they were not registering in my consciousness. Then thoughts began pouring into my head. They were not my thoughts; I had no control over them. I was told three things:

"All your life you have wondered who or what God is, and if he exists. I do exist, and I am Love. Any love you witness for the rest of your life, whether from mother to child or friend to friend, that is me. And I love you.

"You have been asking to be forgiven for this and forgiven for that. I tell you that I forgive you before you ever do the things you need forgiveness for. All you need to be forgiven for is one thing, and you must forgive yourself as I already have. The only gift I have given you is your life, to love and be loved and to love yourself. And you have not done that. I love you unconditionally and forgive you unconditionally. Love yourself and forgive yourself.

"During the rest of your life here, you will have times when you doubt this experience you are now having. You will say you were in a nut ward and you were brainwashed; that this was a psychotic trick of your mind. But you will always be sure of one thing: you will know that for five minutes of your life, you were completely, one-hundred-percent sure that what you were witnessing was true and real. You will be more sure about this experience than you are sure the people you relate this experience to are really there in front of you."

Then the presence left, and I heard the minister say "Amen." I sobbed uncontrollably for thirty minutes or more. I've never felt more humble, loved, or worthy before that moment or since.

So, was this my spiritual awakening? No. Not hardly. Thirty days later I was off in my addiction again, more miserable than ever. I spent years professing that this experience had done nothing for me, as evidenced by the tortured existence I struggled through after that. One thing I could not do, though, was to repeat the old stand-bys I once used when life was hard: "God doesn't love me" or "There is no God."

Now, I know that experience dramatically altered my life and led me to where I am today. I've struggled through recovery for some time, through good times and bad, and through fleeting moments of revelation where I felt that presence again, but this time within myself. Today, I stand in the middle of a full-fledged spiritual awakening. I have begun working the Steps in earnest, albeit grudgingly. I have begun to follow suggestions provided by other members. I'm beginning to realize that God tapped me on the shoulder that day and told me all I would ever need to know. Now I know that to learn how to apply the great wisdom God revealed to me that day, I need to join my fellows.

I was a loner my entire life. I felt either superior or inferior to others, but never equal. Now I know that the presence I felt outside of myself that day is within me and within you. Only together can we unlock our disease's grip on that presence and allow it to manifest itself in our lives. Now, growing weary of depression, loneliness, and pain, I am ready to reach out to you and ask for your help. I desperately need it.

Spiritual awakening? Mine began when I was born. When, as a child, I withdrew from the ugly world because I was different than everyone else. I was awakening that day in high school when I decided there was a God but that he hated me, and took off down the glory road to an addictive life. When I got married. When I got divorced. When I graduated from college. And when I was locked up in a mental hospital. Since I know God loves me unconditionally, I know everything that has happened in my life has happened just the way it was supposed to in order to lead me to where I am right now.

A power that loves me with the love I felt for those five minutes would never allow me to face something I can't handle. It would never allow anything to happen to me unless it would help in my awakening. And I know that my Higher Power patiently and lovingly awaits my willingness to take Step Three, allowing it to give me all the love I could ever dream of.

Thank you, my new friends in OA. Thank you for reaching out even though I slapped your hand. Thank you for loving me when I didn't feel worthy and didn't want your love. Thank you for being there whenever I decided to show up. Thank you for penetrating the thick walls that years of hatred and isolation had built around my spirit inside. I pray that whenever I see a member who is unapproachable, who never smiles, who sends out glares intended to scare others away, that I will see myself. That I will see that lonely frightened me, with those same thick walls. That I will reach out as you have, offer my love and say, "Keep coming back."

I believe that if you are alive, you are having a spiritual awakening. Let's all help each other learn that our good times, and supposed bad times, are all important to us, as we awaken to our true spiritual selves. And when it says in the Big Book at the end of "A Vision for You," "May God bless you and keep you until then," remember: then is now.

— *Colorado USA*

## Coming to Know God

After over a year in OA, I was diligent about working all the tools of recovery, but I felt that something was missing. I was aware that meditation is mentioned in Step Eleven, but since it wasn't one of the tools, I didn't pay too much attention to it.

"God could and would if he were sought" is one of the promises of the program. God could restore me to sanity, if I would seek him. But where, when, and how can I seek God?

If I want a relationship with God, I must do exactly what I do when I want relationships with people: I have to spend time with him, talk to him, listen to him. When I take quiet time only with him, and nobody disturbs us, I can be completely honest. I can share my best and my worst.

It doesn't matter where I do this. Wherever I am, I can visualize whatever kind of place I prefer. The important thing is that I am quiet enough to consciously put myself in his presence, seeking his will for me; I ask for his guidance and protection.

When I didn't know God yet, I had to act as if I knew him. Slowly, I came to know my nourishing, loving, caring God, who works with me and loves me unconditionally. He encourages rather than threatens.

I could not have the recovery I have today if it weren't for God. And I couldn't have the relationship I have with God without the time I spend in meditation.

— *Wisconsin USA*

# Positive Higher Power

My search for God began with a conversation I had with my old sponsor. I told him I was having a hard time with the whole idea of surrendering control of my life to a power greater than myself. It wasn't the surrender I had such difficulty with; it was believing that this "Higher Power" would actually be able to do anything in my life.

You know, all I ever wanted was to find something that could make me feel better about myself. Nothing I tried worked for very long, though. My sponsor called these my negative higher powers. After all, he said, I had a lot of experience using higher powers to make my life more tolerable; but in the end, I always wound up in a worse situation than when I started. So, my problem was not whether I believed that a higher power could work, but which one. He told me to stop using all those negative higher powers and begin to use the one suggested in the Big Book. Or I could choose one of my own. The point was that I needed to start somewhere.

*I had to begin by scrapping my old ideas about what God was supposed to do for me.*

If you think that came at all easily to me, I have some oceanfront property in Nevada I'd like to sell you. It was the hardest thing I've ever done, and I'm still doing it. I had to begin by scrapping all of my old ideas about what God was supposed to do for me, and what I was supposed to do for God. We each had a part to play in this relationship. What arrogance it was to think I could determine what God's responsibilities were in my life! When I went to the Big Book, I found out what *my* duties were, not God's.

The book said that my sole purpose for living is to do God's will in my life and help my fellow man. That was as clear to me as mud. I discovered that it didn't matter to God where I worked, as long as it was something I could do well and it kept me out of jail. He wanted me to be happy in my work and to give an honest day's work for an honest day's pay. I cannot expect to receive first-class wages for second- or third-class production; that wouldn't be honest. And dishonesty is not God's will for any of us.

My duties in my relationship with God are fairly clear to me now. I need to live without harming myself or others as much as possible, and I need to be of maximum service to my fellows. That does not mean I need to be a doormat. There are people in this world who will treat me without respect, no matter how I treat them. I don't have to try to change their minds, but neither do I need to treat them as they treat me. I need to love them as they are, not as I would have them be. I am here to try to understand, rather than to be understood; and to love, rather than to be loved. I'm not always successful in treating everyone with the dignity and respect they deserve, but I'm trying.

God does not need me to tell him whether he is doing his job well. Rather, I need to be on the lookout for areas in my life where selfishness and self-centeredness start creeping in. I need to be aware of my motives in my dealings with others. If I'm trying to meet a need through manipulation, I will pay a penalty for those actions, and so will those around me. Eventually, I will climb back up on the pot of self-pity, and there is only room for one up there. I will, once again, be alone in a misery of my own making.

Isn't it ironic that when I gave up trying to get the things in life I thought I deserved, I got all the things that make me happy? The harder I tried to make those things happen, the more they eluded me. All this improvement comes to me slowly and with a lot of emotional upheaval. (Notice that I use the present tense; it is still happening.) There are times when I just want the feelings to stop, but I realize that no growth happens without discomfort. And the joy on the other side of the growth makes me want more.

I am convinced that God's will for each and every one of us is to be happy in our lives and to share that growth with others.

— *Georgia USA*

# A Self-Chosen Concept

When I was a child, people around me loved to tell me what my concept of God should be. For me, there were two things wrong with this. First, it gave me an image of a jealous, demanding, judgmental God, certainly not a source of unconditional love. Second, because I hated being told what to think, it aroused feelings of criticism and rebellion in me. The boy scientist that I was couldn't fail to notice holes in the logic of so many religious stories. As a result, my spiritual pursuits as an adult never resulted in closeness to a Higher Power. I never found a God I could talk to and listen to.

But OA is unique. You told me to find a Higher Power of my own understanding, emphasizing that to do so was a life-and-death matter. You silenced the inner critic forever. How can I criticize a concept I've made and understood myself and am free to modify at any time?

> *I seemed unchanged, but it seemed that everyone around me was having a spiritual awakening.*

At last I was able to feel closeness to a power greater than myself. I felt that I actually had a chance at true happiness. From that moment, my gradual spiritual awakening began. Like many of us, I was slow in noticing it. I seemed unchanged to myself, but it seemed that everyone around me was having a spiritual awakening.

Before OA, my efforts at meditation were mostly disappointing. I was never able to clear my mind. Whenever my thought process would stop, a mental visualization took its place. The void was denied me. But at an OA retreat, an experienced meditator gave me validation; he said that focusing on an inspiring mental image was a perfectly valid, even excellent, meditation technique. I had been doing it right, after all!

So visualizing during meditation became my way of staying close to my Higher Power. I knew my concept of a Higher Power was feminine, but I needed a specific image.

For the first time, I looked at a statue in my bedroom with my mind free of prior religious programming. I saw a female figure of super-human proportions, with a face that expresses the essence of unconditional love and compassion. For most of my day, I am a responsible adult. But for those few moments of meditation, I am a child at peace, safe in his mother's arms.

— *California USA*


# What Does God Call You?

I was talking with a sponsoree recently, and our conversation got to the heart of the OA program: God as we understand God. My friend was pretty terrified by the holiness of God. She felt inadequate, undeserving, detached from her creator.

Somewhat like my sponsoree, I had been taught as a child to set myself apart from a supreme being who was omnipotent, who could do everything I could not. I was afraid of someone so perfect, whose perfection I was urged to adore, while I was miserably lonely and starving for acceptance. Perhaps I got a little, but it wasn't enough, or it was always mingled with criticism and correction. I remember more severity than merriment.

Many of us in OA were urged by parents or teachers to pray to such a being for help; or, if we did not have religious training, God was the one we asked for help in times of crisis: Don't let my sister die; save me from financial ruin; don't let my dad hurt me again.

Somehow, for many of us who approach recovery willingly and with hope, that concept of God—not as a loving Higher Power but as Almighty Warrior Who Has It In For Us—has remained to torment us.

After the Step work of surrendering our compulsive overeating and our unmanageable lives, after an examination of character defects and a willingness to be changed and to live in "a new freedom and a new happiness," we can still be scared silly. A frightening, overbearing, judging God is still the director in some people's minds. Such a concept can wither the heart. Fear is a human condition, or we would not be always praying for "courage to change the things we can."

I suggested that my friend picture God as loving. I asked her to imagine God's hands as the hands of a careful artist who would no more bruise a child's skin than produce bad art. (A prayerful look at nature proves that God is no bad artist!) Can you allow God to call you "darling," I asked her; "little one" or "sweetheart?" Can you be the child who gladdens your Higher Power's heart at the mere sight of you? Can you conceive of God as a great heart rather than a great punisher?

If I nourish this concept of a Higher Power who sweet-talks my starved ears and heart, I grow more certain that God's kindness is a gift I can claim, that I am deeply lovable and worthy of gentle treatment. So many people can be bathed in the light of one generous smile. How many more of us (babies at heart) could bask in the accepting glow of a God who says, "You, dear heart, are the light of my life!"

A gentle-handed being is my concept of God. This understanding always settles me into a sense of peace and trust—a gentle awareness of my connection to other people here on earth. I ate compulsively for years over the fear and guilt I inherited from the traditional religion of my childhood. Today, God the quiet, the nurturing, the lover of peace—the one who calls me "sweetheart"—is always at my side. God's will be done.

— *Ohio USA*

# Only Seventy Days

My OA life is only seventy days young. Still, I feel qualified to write a letter to *Lifeline* as part of my service.

For over forty years my life was totally unmanageable when it came to food. In addition, many other areas were unmanageable too. I was all but dead seventy days ago, still going through the motions and pretending I could handle life. Only I knew the truth: I was ruined. I'd lost my husband to deceit. I'd lost my son to despair and lies. I'd lost my home through deception. I'd lost my God because I couldn't believe he truly existed. I had no income.

When I walked through the doors of my first OA meeting, I thought it was all or nothing. Since I felt I had lost everything anyway, why not just give up? But I listened, hanging on by a thread, and I heard the words I needed to hear that night. I heard: Get a sponsor as fast as you can. So I did. I heard: Get a starter packet and a Twelve-Step book. I did these things too. I heard: Pick up a hotline sheet before you leave, and so I did that. I heard: Grant me the serenity to accept what I can't change, and I asked those members' HP to become mine as well. He did. I asked him to make me feel satisfied eating just the right amount at my meals. He did that for me too. I asked not to be isolated any longer. I asked and he responded, each day and each night. I confessed: you are a power greater than I am. And now I wonder, why was there ever any doubt?

> *This HP is waiting to hear from you, as he so patiently waited for me.*

As I write this, I know this HP is waiting to hear from you, as he so patiently waited for me until seventy days ago.

— *Anonymous*

# Transcendence Is Spiritual

I came to OA six and a half years ago as a broken, hopelessly depressed woman. I could not stop my compulsive eating. At almost five feet tall (152 cm), I came closer to 200 pounds (91 kg) than I had ever expected to be.

The meeting that night gave me the first glimmer of hope I'd had in years. Two days later I found my first sponsor, became abstinent, and have remained so ever since. I have maintained a 70-pound (32-kg) weight loss all this time.

*Our path in OA transcends weight loss and a return to emotional health.*

My spiritual recovery is one of the many miracles of OA. It allowed me to reclaim the parts of myself that had remained deeply hidden because of shame and the fear of being different. I now feel a great sense of rightness about the religion of my childhood, and I understand that our path in OA transcends weight loss (physical recovery) and a return to emotional health. We find transcendence in the spiritual path.

For me that means I have the freedom to choose the path, the willingness to explore it, and the ability to set limits on how far to travel. The OA program teaches me to take one day at a time. If I wish to practice a religion to enhance my spiritual growth, it's entirely up to me. My Higher Power will lead me where I need to be.

It's all found in the promises in the Big Book. One step at a time, one day at a time. When I first came into program, it was difficult for me to say out loud the word "God"! Now, God and I are always together, one step at a time. Thank you, God.

— *Massachusetts USA*

# My Journey to Belief

When I came to my first OA meeting twenty years ago, I was angry at God. I had prayed for my husband to quit drinking about fifteen years earlier, and I became angry when God didn't give me what I asked. I had never before prayed for anything for myself. How dare God not give me what I asked!

My growth in this program has been slow. In the beginning, I'm sure it was because every time I heard the word God, I wanted to get up and leave the meeting. But I was thoroughly defeated. I didn't know what else to do. I kept coming back because I wanted to lose weight and be happy. I saw this happening in other people's lives in OA, and I wanted it for myself.

I was miserable when I came to OA. My husband and I were not getting along; my older son was not speaking to me; my younger son was in the Navy (in the Philippines); I detested my boss. I had nothing positive in my life.

After a year of going to meetings off and on, I got to Step Two at a retreat. I came to believe that a power greater than myself could restore me to sanity. At that point, the power still was not God, but my OA group, the people in OA, and my sponsor. It took me another year to get to Step Three, when I was willing to turn my will and my life over to God. I still didn't see God as this wonderful entity to take care of me, but I didn't think God could be any worse at handling things than I was.

After I took my first Fourth and Fifth Steps, I began to accept that God loved me just as I was. It didn't matter that I was not perfect and I would never be perfect. I also got involved in service beyond my group level.

I believe it was working the Steps to the best of my ability, and service, that helped me see God as a kind, loving entity who only wanted the best for me and for all of his children. It was then that I fired the judgmental God of my childhood who was always out to get me. I now have a God who is a friend I can count on. I believe the only people who fail in Twelve-Step programs are those who leave. I did not come to this program to find God, but that is what happened as a result of working the Twelve Steps. I am very grateful that I didn't leave before the miracle happened to me.

Keep coming back. It works.

*— Minnesota USA*

# The Miracle of Belief

I am a grateful, recovering compulsive eater and bulimic. I never want to forget who I am. For a long time I tried to be a normal eater. Only by accepting who I am did I find peace.

I've been in program for eleven years and I've been binge-free for ten years. I recently celebrated that miraculous anniversary by going back to my original home meeting and sharing my hope with those present. Much has changed since my first meeting so many years ago.

*I had a Higher Power. Unfortunately, that power was food.*

The most wonderful change has been my spirituality. When I came into the rooms, I had a Higher Power. Unfortunately, that power was food, and the God of my understanding wasn't much help. I believed in God, but I certainly did not trust God. I am one of those people who had to "come to believe." I kept coming back. I listened, and marveled at the people who could eat a meal and stop: I wanted what they had. I wanted so badly to "get it." Others told me it was a gift from my Higher Power, the one that wouldn't grant my laundry list of requests. Why should God give me this gift now?

I kept coming back, and I started working the Steps with a sponsor. I realized the problem was not that God was noncompliant, but that I needed to change. As a result of doing an inventory, I saw that my character defects were standing in the way of a joyous, free, and happy life. Now I had to turn to this God and ask for these defects to be removed. I had asked for so many things that were not granted in the past. Why would God relieve me of my defects and the compulsion to overeat?

I've learned the magic of letting go and accepting. I've learned that I cannot blame my human limitations on my Higher Power. I've learned that the God of my understanding is kind, gentle, forgiving, feminine, unconditionally loving, and trustworthy. I've learned that God never says no, but rather yes, not yet, or I've got something better.

The Steps gave me the freedom to have a God I can trust and believe in. As a result, the compulsion to binge has been lifted and my plan of eating has been refined over the years. I've been transformed so that I want to believe I've been created to reflect God's image—the new image I can understand.

Because I believe in that transformation, I came to believe I could be a good parent and pass on a healthy way of life. This is the most recent miracle in my life. I've been blessed with an abstinent pregnancy, the natural delivery of a beautiful baby girl, and the willingness to stay abstinent so I can feel all the comfortable and uncomfortable feelings this child's presence has evoked.

The newest challenge will be learning to balance caring for myself and caring for this child. As long as I take direction from my Higher Power, I know I will be shown the way. What a difference letting go and letting God has made in my life. I am forever grateful to OA.

— *Pennsylvania USA*

# God with Skin On

Ionce heard a story in church about a little boy who was afraid of the dark. His dad tucked him into bed one night, said goodnight and turned off the light. But each time the father tried to leave, the little boy came up with some excuse to get his dad to stay a few minutes longer: a goodnight kiss, a drink of water, a final trip to the potty. Finally, in desperation, the child told his father that he was afraid to stay in the room by himself. His father said, exasperated, "Don't be afraid, son, God is in here with you." The reply: "Well, could you stay in here, too? Tonight I think I need somebody with skin on."

*God puts skin on and comes to me in the form of other OA members.*

Sometimes I think I need a God with skin on too. Especially when I feel alone with my troubles. In those times, God puts skin on and comes to comfort me in the form of other OA members. When I am hurting, struggling, sad, angry, or lonely, I call someone from OA and I always find relief. Someone is on the other end to listen to me, share his or her experience, and offer hope. They let me cry and say silly, irrational things. They tell me that this, too, shall pass; that I don't have to eat over it; that God loves me; and that things will get better. Their words are like salve on my aching emotions. I find myself comforted and able to breathe again, and then I can figure out what actions I need to take next. I feel as if I've been sitting in my Higher Power's lap, with my head tucked under his chin, wrapped in his arms, listening to his heartbeat. It's a wonderful feeling.

As I experience the love and acceptance of other recovering compulsive overeaters, I'm learning to understand what God is really like. He knows that sometimes the best way to comfort his hurting child is to use another of his children; that sometimes the only thing we need to know is that someone else has been where we are, understands, and has made it out just fine. A God like this is trustworthy, and it's slowly becoming easier to turn my will and my life—especially around food—over to him. God is not out to get me, after all! In my hardest times he proves most gentle and caring.

After several years, I continue to work this program, learning about God as I experience his qualities in other people. I guess we never know when we will be "God with skin on." One of the miracles of this program is that struggling compulsive overeaters who feel hopeless become useful within our Fellowship. Just by listening to someone on the phone; sponsoring him or her; or sharing before, during, or after a meeting, I may be sharing God's love at the very moment that person needs to feel it. I may unknowingly say exactly what the person needs to hear—just like when I call someone and that person does the same for me.

Suddenly, answering the phone and making phone calls look more important. I see sharing before and after the meeting in a whole new light. Writing an article is more of a joy, because I never know when I will be God's "skin"!

— *Virginia USA*

# God and I Together

I had an active religious upbringing, yet I never felt I truly belonged. Higher Power (whom I call God) was a domineering, paternalistic, demanding, impossibly perfect God, requiring contradictory actions from me, "or else." I was scared to death of God. I ate to escape my shame and to seek from food the comfort that God didn't give me.

I searched for a new relationship with God in many different religious pursuits, and even looked to atheism as an answer to the God issue. But that didn't work because I had an inner awareness or belief in God. At this point, I believed that God was a malicious practical joker, playing games with my life and laughing at me while I struggled. God was "on high": outside of me, unavailable, and unfriendly.

Then, through my Twelve-Step recovery, I developed a personal relationship with God and learned to turn my will and life over to God's care. In my ten-plus years in OA, this relationship has taken on a new intensity. God works in my life, not just observes.

Before coming to OA, I had gained and lost over 1,500 pounds (682 kg), with a top weight of 320 pounds (145 kg) and a low weight of 155 pounds (70 kg). When I came to OA in 1988, I struggled for two years to get abstinent and gained weight up to 272 pounds (124 kg). With my initial abstinence, I didn't gain any more weight for four years. I was ecstatic about that, although like any overweight person, I wanted to be thin. I was no longer bingeing, and it felt great.

Then, by not going to meetings, not doing service, not reading literature, and not writing, I talked myself into relapse and went back on the weight-loss-and-gain merry-go-round from hell. I stayed there for four years, all the while maintaining a superficial relationship with God and OA.

> I did my part and trusted God to do his part— my weight loss.

Finally, because of God working through another OA member who offered to sponsor me, I have again achieved abstinence. I am again ecstatic not to be bingeing. This time, however, I used all the tools and now have a 71-pound (32-kg) weight loss and a deeper relationship with God. This came about by using the tools of abstinence—plan of eating, meetings, service, sponsorship, literature, writing, anonymity, and phone calls. I did my part and trusted God to do his part—my weight loss.

God has taught me abundance, moderation, trust, self-esteem, and serenity. All of this was possible only through working the Twelve Steps of OA while staying abstinent and using the tools. I was willing to go to any length for recovery.

Yes, God works in my life today, and I am grateful to God and OA for my recovery from compulsive overeating. I had to take action (meetings, Step work, calling in my food) and trust God to take the weight. God did, and I have changed, as has my concept of a Higher Power.

— *Washington USA*

# Key to My Heart

When I first came to Overeaters Anonymous in 1984, I had a negative concept of God and I was angry at him. For this reason, I initially saw the love, tolerance, and support of my OA group as my Higher Power. As time went on, I became more open to change and able to share my feelings with a sponsor. I knew that if I wanted to truly believe a power greater than myself could restore me to sanity (Step Two), I needed a more tangible concept of my Higher Power. I shared with my sponsor that I didn't like the God I believed existed. My sponsor shared how she used to have negative feelings about God, so she decided to "fire" the God of her past and "hire" a new one. At my sponsor's instructions, I wrote a job description of the God I wanted. He had to love me unconditionally and accept me with my faults. He had to be my friend, never leave my side, have a sense of humor, and never punish people with bad things. After I wrote this, my sponsor and I symbolically burned the "job application" to confirm that the vacancy had been filled.

The ritual was nice, but I didn't really believe it. I asked my sponsor what I could do to make it a reality. Her response resulted in the most profound miracle of my life. My sponsor said, "Act as if you believe, and some day the desire will become reality." Because I trusted my sponsor and wanted the kind of recovery I saw in her, I acted as if I had a loving God in my life. Eventually, in conjunction with my own spiritual awakening, the desire became reality.

I have used the "act as if" concept in many aspects of my OA growth. The most remarkable use, for which I will always be grateful to God, resulted in a change in my relationship with my mother. When I came to OA, I blamed my mother for many things I felt were wrong with me, and I greatly disliked this woman. As I recovered through the Twelve Steps, especially as a result of Steps Four and Nine, I let go of my resentment and realized that my mother had her own baggage and had done the best she could. Yet, I still could not feel love for her. I felt concern, and responsibility for her well-being, but I could not feel love. This bothered me, especially when purchasing Mother's Day, birthday, and Christmas cards. It was difficult to find cards that weren't full of sentiments I didn't feel.

A few years ago, I attended a retreat led by a long-time OA member whose recovery I admired. In the course of her sharing, she explained how at one point she had hated her mother. Through the Steps, she had let go of those feelings. She shared the difficulty of buying greeting cards because they all contained expressions of love she did not feel. As a result of program, she reached a point where she did feel love for her mother and did not feel like a phony expressing this sentiment. During the first session break, I approached the leader to ask what she had done to get to the point of love. Her answer was, "I acted as if." She explained that rather than feeling hypocritical buying cards that expressed love, she bought them and acted as if she believed their sentiments. At some point she realized that she was no longer acting. The miracle had happened, and she did feel love for her mother.

Putting my newly learned concept into action, I started buying cards that expressed love and other feelings I wished I felt for my mother. Then I worked on acting as if I loved her. On the Saturday before Mother's Day 1997, I flew out of state to visit my mother at her nursing home. I gave her a Mother's Day card, thanked her for all the care she had given me, and said, "I love you." When I reached down to hug her, it happened. I knew I really did love her! I no longer had to act. Little did I know it would be my last chance to tell my mother in person that I loved her. Six months later I received a call saying she had died in her sleep.

Thank God for Overeaters Anonymous, where I've learned to be a better person. I am thankful for all the wonderful OA people who have been willing to share their experience so I can learn and grow. I will always be especially grateful to that retreat leader, who gave me the key that opened my heart to my mother.

— *Massachusetts USA*


## Zapped with the Spirit

Working the OA program has brought peace and serenity into my life. When I think of serenity, the words that come to mind are peaceful, tranquil, unruffled, placid, calm, and clear-minded.

I haven't spent most of my life feeling peaceful. Instead, I felt I had to control everything around me. I had opinions about everything, which I held to and defended no matter what the cost or outcome.

*I hit an emotional and spiritual bottom three years ago when I realized how unmanageable my life had become.*

I hit an emotional and spiritual bottom three years ago when I realized how unmanageable my life had become. That's when I came through the doors of OA. I put on a good front, but had no inner peace. I carried longstanding resentments toward several people and some family members. Shortly after starting to work the Twelve Steps, I was zapped with a spiritual awakening. As a result I quit the debating society, putting aside my opinions and self-will. I can't describe the peace of mind I've had since I learned that serenity is more important than having my way.

I realized that I could choose my moods and thoughts. I could choose to put love, peace, gentleness, and kindness at the center of my being, so that warmth and cheer would extend to those I meet. However, first I had to learn how to keep my serenity.

When I turned my will and my life over to God, my first reward was a miraculous, unprecedented peace of mind and soul. God changed my life through working the Twelve Steps of OA. It is truly a miracle. I find that it's impossible to keep this peace and serenity to myself. It shines from deep inside me with little effort.

The other important factor in my newfound peace is the joy of forgiveness and making amends. God has taught me that I'm responsible only for what I do and say.

I am not responsible for, nor can I control, how others treat me. I am responsible for keeping my side of the fence clean. If I do that daily, making amends as I go, I don't collect the old baggage of bad feelings and the discontent they bring.

When God came into my life a few years ago, I had many amends to make for past wrongs. I even had to forgive people who had done me wrong, but who had never asked for forgiveness and never would. That's not easy to do, but I had to do it to be free of my lifelong resentments. Thankfully, God guided me through every Step.

How do I maintain inner peace? I give everything to God: my fears, worries, and life. I know I'll never be perfect, so I trust my bank of good will with those who know me, knowing I can draw on it when I slip.

— *Ontario, Canada*

# Finding a New God

I grew up in a family that went to church on Sunday and said a rote prayer before family meals. God was not mentioned in a positive way at any other time. The only reference I remember hearing was "God punishes little girls who ..." (fill in the blank with anything my mom didn't like).

That thought occurred to me recently when I changed to a quicker line in a supermarket, and the one I changed to started moving more slowly. I thought, "See, God punishes little girls who are in a hurry." When that thought crossed my mind, I chuckled to myself because that is definitely NOT the God I believe in since coming to OA.

The God I believe in today wants what is best for me and is infinitely patient when I make mistakes. It is not a God who is a super accountant, keeping a record of everything I do wrong. It is a God who gently encourages me to do better, who lifts me up and carries me when I fall. It is a God who understands and encourages my humanness, while leading me to grow in my recovery. It is a God who is kind, loving, encouraging, and patient—a God who puts wonderful people and events in my life and wants me to take advantage of them. It is a God

*God is not a super accountant, keeping a record of everything I do wrong.*

who yearns to give me my "heart's desires" as I continue to work my OA program, seeking to improve my conscious contact with him so I can better know and do his will.

— *Louisiana USA*

# Steps to Spiritual Awakening

It was time to write on Step Twelve again, and again I was asking, "What spiritual awakening?" I picked up my pen and started to remember and write.

In Step One, I recognized and came to believe that food was my Higher Power. Not that I expected food to work miracles for me, but I did use it to buffer my emotions. I'm happy—eat. Poor me—eat. Food would make me feel better. It didn't work anymore, but I couldn't see that. Food buffered my feelings; therefore, my life became unmanageable. Just as it is hard to drive a car with insulated mittens, it was hard to live so deeply muffled.

In Step Two, I saw the futility of making food my God, so I had to look elsewhere. First, I looked to the group and my sponsor, and eventually to their beliefs and practices. Slowly the power of OA became real, believable, and even possible for me. By doing as they did, I might change as they had changed. Hope was born.

*I hadn't run my life well; maybe HP and OA could do better.*

In Step Three, I jumped in. I took a sponsor, became abstinent, and started to work the Steps on paper. I defined God. I hadn't run my life well; maybe HP and OA could do better.

In Steps Four and Five, I saw much as I wrote my inventory. Still, it took a while to sink in. Not until Step Five did my defects become real. The exact nature of my wrongs became apparent as I shared my inventory and realized how much time I had spent taking other people's inventories.

By Step Six, I wanted to wake up a saint. No work; no worries. I felt ready, but didn't act ready. I wasn't ready to try to change my life by replacing the old ways with new ways. I was still trying to wish my way through life.

By Step Seven, I thought I was humble. I was begging to have my shortcomings taken from me—now! To me, the word "humbly" almost denies asking. When God is ready, he will take them away if I will let them go.

In Steps Eight and Nine, I made a list of all persons I had known. I still had (have) quite an ego. My sponsor and I worked through the list one by one. I made some amends and let go of others. A new way of living emerged as the old baggage was removed. I could remove a resentment as soon as I saw it, so it wouldn't fester and poison me. Though much of me was still old, the new slowly became stronger. Life became worth living again.

Step Ten is like a daily vitamin pill. It improves the quality of my life. I can skip it now and then with no apparent loss. Yet, I am healthier if I partake of its blessings daily.

Step Eleven is a humility-enhancing, ego-reducing Step. I need to seek God's will and request his power. As I seek, I remember that it's not up to me to fix, control, help, or direct the world. I am best and happiest when I can see myself as God's tool. When I don't fight the flow, I can just be.

So there is my spiritual awakening. It surprises me that I still have to look for it. It amazes me that when I do look for it, I find it. All I need to do now is share it.

— *Illinois USA*

# CHAPTER TWO

# Turning Our Lives and Our Will Over to a Higher Power

*It isn't easy to hand control over to HP, but these*
*OA members found that the program would work*
*only if they did so.*

# A Program Barometer

It's been twelve years since I attended my first OA meeting. There have been many phases in my recovery: gratifying growth leaps, as well as small and even large steps backward. Today I can honestly say I'm grateful for being a compulsive overeater, and that's why I'm writing this article.

During my years in program, I've been fortunate to experience recovery on all three levels: physical, emotional, and spiritual. All are important, but at different times one aspect has taken priority over another. Now I believe my Higher Power is guiding me to focus on my spirituality.

When I first came to the program I'd had no experience with religion or spirituality. I was one of those people who had to start out considering the group to be my Higher Power. Hundreds of meetings and thousands of pages of literature later, I find myself reaping the benefits of a conscious relationship with the God of my understanding.

During the past six months, my spiritual growth has accelerated, which has been most challenging for me. As I stretch myself in this area, I find I am susceptible to my default emotion of fear. And I'm so concerned about doing God's will that I've fallen back into unhealthy patterns of self-criticism. I abuse myself with thoughts that I'm just not doing it well enough.

Then I had a revelation that renewed my gratitude for my disease. I realized that, unlike normal people, we compulsive overeaters have a handy, tangible barometer. If I want to know whether I'm doing God's will, all I have to do is observe what I'm eating. No matter what my head tells me about what I am or am not doing, if my food is clean, I'm on the right track! I still have my ups and downs both in moods and productivity, but remaining abstinent is all I need to do. Everything else will fall into place according to God's plan.

— *California USA*

# Living Every Day as It Comes

New Year's Day has always been difficult for me. I would make a zillion resolutions and break them all within a week. Losing weight was always at the very top of the list, of course. Sound familiar? Now I see the insanity of it all. A compulsive person has no business making resolutions. Why? Why can't I be like the rest of the world in this respect? After three years in recovery, the answer is clear to me.

When I make resolutions, I am taking back control over the most important things in my life. This immediately puts me in a vulnerable position, because taking my life into my own hands means I must let go of God's hand. When I take control away from God, my recovery is at risk. My program begins to unravel. Emotional and physical abstinence become more elusive the harder I try to hang on to them. It's a cycle I know well.

*Taking my life into my own hands means I must let go of God's hand.*

Now I know I have another choice. First, I don't have to make New Year's Day such a big deal. Like all holidays, New Year's is filled with hype, but I can choose how to participate. I can simply acknowledge that the old year is coming to a close and a new one is here. I take a moment to thank my Higher Power for all he's done for me in the past year; it's a good time for a gratitude list. I used to spend New Year's Eve dwelling on my failures and planning how I could "do better" next year. This time, I can dwell on the good things and be grateful for them.

Next, instead of making empty resolutions such as "lose weight," "be a nicer person" or "manage money more wisely," I can simply renew my commitment to my recovery program, to my Higher Power, and to the Twelve Steps. By working the Steps, I know my life will be just as it's supposed to be.

This year when someone asks what resolutions I've made, I can smile and say, "Oh, I've made only one, and that is to not make any resolutions." I can go about my new year doing the things my Higher Power has for me to do. I have no way of knowing what's in store for me, and today I am thankful for that. I take joy in living every day as it comes—with tears, laughter, love—and I'm so glad to leave the rest to God. Happy New Year. Happy New Life!

— *Colorado USA*


# Willing to Take Action

I used to think of willingness as passive. Sure, I was willing. I was willing to admit I was powerless over food and that my life was unmanageable. I was willing to believe that a Power greater than myself could restore me to sanity. I was willing to turn my will and my life over to ANY power that would lift my merciless obsession with food and make me a normal eater. Those were the first three Steps, right?

I remember the first time I read that Step Three was an action Step. I could not understand that. I was willing to turn my will and my life over to a Higher Power, but I was not willing to take any responsibility for it. "Okay, HP, you got me. I'm all yours." That was as far as I got my first time around with the Steps. But when God didn't instantly remove my obsession with food, and when he didn't turn me into a normal eater, I got angry. Why wasn't this program working?

Today I can accept responsibility for myself. I have to be willing to take action. I have to be willing to admit I am powerless over food and then DO something about it. Today, that means I need to create a plan of eating. I need to call my sponsor to help me stay on track. I need to go to meetings and pray and meditate to stay in touch with my Higher Power. All of these require willingness through action.

Today I am willing to let God restore me to sanity. This means I pick up a pen and start writing when I get the food thoughts. It means that when I think I can skip a meeting, I go anyway. It means that I pray instead of breaking my commitment to my plan of eating. I have to be willing to ask. God has never turned me down when I ask for help. Yet, sometimes I refuse to ask.

For today, I am willing. Willingness is a gift from God as a result of working this program. I am grateful for the willingness to do whatever it takes to recover from this disease today.

— *Missouri USA*

## Complete Confidence in God

People generally speak of faith in conjunction with religion and spiritual emotions, as a belief in an unknown happening, emotion, or state of consciousness. Faith in conjunction with the OA program begins with Step Three, but can be found hidden in all Twelve Steps.

Making a decision to turn our will and our lives over to the care of God is an act of faith. I came to believe in a power greater than myself through the Twelve Steps. OA has brought a new commitment to my life. I've found complete confidence in this organization, its beliefs, and its principles. This commitment brings me to faith in my Higher Power. OA has brought me a deeper understanding of my own religious beliefs and has increased my awareness of my spirituality. This creates a bond between my faith in a Higher Power and my OA program.

I found faith in the belief that my Higher Power would allow me to feel my emotions safely if I did not stuff them down again with food. To feel my emotions, sometimes for the very first time, was a step in faith, moving me into recovery.

- Step One gave me faith that I could find help for my unmanageable life by admitting I was a compulsive overeater.

- Step Two contains faith as a commitment to believe in a Higher Power.

- Step Three, as an action of turning over my will, is the ultimate act of faith.

- Step Four's inventory requires faith in my ability to look into my past honestly.

- Step Five is a leap of faith in confiding to another person my past transgressions, sins, and fantasies, and all of my actions, both good and bad.

- Step Six has been the trickiest Step in faith for me, where I had to act as if I were entirely ready to have my defects removed. How could I be sure? Faith.

- Step Seven is a commitment to work together with my Higher Power to overcome my character defects. The deal is that my Higher Power will remove my defects, and I commit, in faith, not to take them back.

- Step Eight teaches faith that God can rectify the faults of my own making, as I become willing to make amends.

- Step Nine, when I make my amends, holds faith that God can help others accept my apologies.

- Step Ten bears the faith that a continued inventory and journaling will help me grow strong and hold the Twelve Steps in my heart.

- Step Eleven brings faith that I can meet my Higher Power with joy in prayer and meditation.

- Step Twelve is faith that I can share and help save others from the pitfalls of our disease, with God's help.

Gratitude is the final aspect of faith. Without gratitude, faith means nothing. Without recognizing the wonderful accomplishments of my Higher Power, I could easily slip back into my ego and self-centeredness, believing that I accomplished all of this on my own. Thank you, Dear Sweet God, for allowing me to share my faith and belief in you.

*— Florida USA*

## Putting Things in Perspective

I have been in Overeaters Anonymous for almost twenty-four years, and my attitude toward many things has changed over that period, especially lately. When I first came into OA, I assumed, as most assume, that the reason I came was to lose weight. Therefore, the so-called physical part of the program was the most important. After many years of living in recovery, my perspective and priorities have changed.

I came into OA to feel good, and, of course, I thought that losing weight would help me feel good. I know of no one who says, "I feel good; I think I will change." No, we all feel bad about ourselves and our lives, and that is why we are willing to change. We all believe that by losing weight we will feel better. Yet, one of the saddest days of my life was when I reached my goal weight and realized that nothing had changed except my weight. I was still the same person I had always been, and I would always find something to justify feeling bad—if not the weight, then something else. I was addicted to feeling bad and I used my weight to justify that feeling.

*One of the saddest days of my life was when I reached my goal weight and realized that nothing had changed except my weight.*

Now, after all these years in OA and living a program of recovery, I have come face-to-face with reality. My doctor has informed me that I have cancer and the chances of recovery from that disease are very limited. Perhaps I have just a few months.

With cancer, as with my disease of compulsive eating, I must do the footwork and leave the results to God. Since I've learned to live one day at a time through OA, those words now take on a different meaning.

Each day I look at what is important for that day and, with the help of my sponsor, my OA friends, my wife, and my Higher Power, I am able to succeed.

When I first read the Big Book, it struck me that nowhere does it talk about physical recovery, except as a result of God's intervention which comes from living the Twelve Steps. While we have a three-fold illness, we have only a spiritual recovery; the physical and emotional recovery comes automatically because of God's will for us.

I am no longer in charge of the results of my life, only what footsteps I take. The physical recovery, both from my disease of compulsive overeating and my disease of cancer, is in God's hands.

So I pass this message on to my OA friends, new and old: no human power can relieve our disease, but God can and will, if he is sought. The way we seek his help is by giving to others. I give to others my desire to live and, to that end, I will live. How well and how long I live is God's choice, not mine.

The physical recovery is his choice; the spiritual mine.

— *Anonymous*

# In God's Hands

"I offer myself to Thee, to build with me and to do with me as Thou wilt …" So begin my prayers to God each day as I rise, continuing with the Serenity Prayer and others. I practically explode with gratitude, relief, and faith each time I say these prayers, because then I am in God's hands.

Before OA, I suffered from low self-esteem, perceived most things negatively, felt everyone picked on me, and didn't try things because I figured I'd fail anyway. I felt this was normal, and that I was simply a victim of life's unfair dealings. Physically, I was an overweight yo-yo eager to be thin, but feeling like a failure because I couldn't be. The day that changed my life came when I read about getting down on my hands and knees to ask God for the willingness to be abstinent for just one day.

*My life changed when I read about getting down on my hands and knees to ask God for the willingness to be abstinent for just one day.*

The next day I went to a meeting, got a sponsor, and have been abstinent and working the program since then. Today I am a vehicle of God's will. I pray daily to do his will and follow His path so I may share my experience, strength, and hope with others. I understand that I receive every gift so I can share it and pass it on.

Today I am pursuing a professional career in Israel (I am from California). I have greater understanding of myself and others, and never in my wildest dreams did I imagine I would love everyone and every life experience as I do now. I maintain a 60-pound (27-kg) physical recovery, which gives me more energy to ask to do more of God's will. Thank you, God and OA. It works if you work it!

— *Anonymous*

# Assembling Life's Pieces

I've been putting puzzles together. Until recently, I didn't realize that was what I was doing; but puzzle after puzzle, I've been putting my life back together.

When I figured out what was happening, I could look back to when I first came to OA and became abstinent. As I began working the program, pieces of a puzzle appeared and I was able to assemble them. Reviewing that puzzle now, I can see it was a simple and straightforward one, so it didn't offer all the answers I thought it would at the time.

I've come to recognize that as the last piece of the first puzzle was put into place, it forced out yet another, more complicated puzzle to be solved. That has apparently been my pattern as I continue to seek recovery. It's a never-ending process. Each succeeding puzzle is larger, more encompassing, and more intricate than its predecessor.

I must acknowledge the growth each last piece represents. To me, it's been the opposite of "peeling the onion." Rather than removing layers to get to the core of things, solutions add dimension to my identity.

*Each succeeding puzzle is larger, more encompassing, and more intricate than its predecessor.*

After solving many puzzles over the four years I've been in program, I've also come to recognize the fear that can accompany putting the last piece in place. Whoosh! Up comes another, more difficult puzzle to solve. More feelings to deal with. Harder problems to figure out. Seemingly impossible questions to answer.

These times before putting the final piece in place often feel uncomfortably familiar. They remind me of my old dieting days when I would reach a plateau in my weight loss. Nothing was happening.

I felt strangely out of touch and separated from what I then believed was important to me. But my priorities have changed. My Higher Power and abstinence are now at the forefront.

Having faith means remembering that my Higher Power will not give me more than I can handle. In fact, I am grateful that my Higher Power (representing my emotionally absent mother and father) gives me increasingly challenging puzzles to solve. By doing so, my HP shows me I can handle it and validates my worth. My Higher Power gives me reason to reevaluate my own self-esteem, or lack of it.

The growth continues. I have so much more to look forward to. It won't be over as long as I stick with my program of recovery in Overeaters Anonymous.

— *Massachusetts USA*

## Who's the Copilot?

I have been meditating and writing every morning, because I've been told it works for other people. I have been in OA for about ten years and have tried just about everything I've been told to do or have heard other people say has worked for them.

I discovered from the beginning that if I acted as if I absolutely believed everything I heard in OA, my life was manageable and I could remain abstinent. I didn't have to live in the misery of trying to fill that big black hole with food. I learned that God, as I call my Higher Power, would fill it for me with love, kindness, happiness, serenity, and all the other wonderful emotions that only he can give me.

This morning I read the "on awakening" passage from the Big Book, pages 86 to 88; pages 83 and 84 about promises; the "Step Seven Prayer" on page 76; and most important, pages 552 and 553 on resentment (*Alcoholics Anonymous*, 4th ed.). I reread yesterday's and today's passages in *For Today*, and then I wrote how I felt or was feeling about myself yesterday and today. I wrote what I hoped to do today, asking God to guide me. Finally, I wrote how I felt about others to see if I was holding onto resentments.

After finishing my morning meditation, I ate breakfast, asking HP to guide my eating and not let me gulp down my food. I then turned on my computer and started playing solitaire games. This is when the miracle happened. I usually waste time playing three or four different games, but yesterday I promised myself that I would only play each game twice whenever I worked on the computer. I did just that, although I wanted to play more. It was then that I suddenly realized God was working for me. I said to myself, "Gee, it's nice having God as my copilot." Just as quickly, I had to say aloud, "Wrong, it's nice being God's copilot." For it was then I knew that God was really and truly in charge of my life. All I have to do is get the heck out of his way, and then sit back and enjoy the ride.

Thank You, God. Thank you, OA.

— *California USA*

# Keeping the Faith

It's hard to have faith when nothing seems to be going right. I guess that's why it's called faith.

I have been in OA for more than thirteen years, and have been abstinent all that time. Today I find that sometimes the hardest thing for me to do is to have faith.

Several years ago a friend of mine taught me a great lesson. I was feeling depressed and fearful over lack of work. I had just finished a series of jobs, and I found myself staring at a blank calendar that seemed to be saying to me, "You'll never work again." I felt as if my life were over.

I called this friend, and he shared some of his faith with me. He told me that when he starts to feel that way, he prays; but instead of asking God to send him something, he thanks God for all that is on its way to him right now. Then he lets it go.

I tried this. I had nothing to lose; I certainly couldn't feel any worse. I thanked God for all the work he was sending my way. I thanked God for sending me everything I needed. Then I let it go.

Barely thirty minutes later, after receiving a variety of phone calls, I had more work than I could have imagined. It felt like a miracle. It was a miracle. It was faith.

> *I thanked God for sending me everything I needed. Thirty minutes later, I had more work than I could have imagined.*

Every time I learn something new, it's a miracle. It's a miracle that I can be open enough to accept something that hasn't yet been proven to me. That's a form of faith.

When I look at what happened back then, it seems that I was doing the first three Steps. Step One, I am powerless; Step Two, there is a power greater than myself; and Step Three, I am turning my will and my life over to that power.

What was so wonderful to me was that this simple act gave me back my serenity. I could have continued to worry and panic for thirty minutes. Where would it have gotten me? My guess is further into panic.

This event occurred more than ten years ago. I still go through periods of worry and panic; but when I remember to be quiet and meditate, I am reminded that I can thank God for everything that is on its way to me. I can have faith, hope, and peace. I can let God pull me through my problem. It feels much better than trying to punch my way out of it.

— *Anonymous*

# Let God Be God

OA has many slogans that help in our recovery program. "Let go and let God" is one I have relied on to help me with one of my character defects, commonly known as perfectionism.

Being a compulsive person, I hesitated to try anything unless I could do it perfectly, or at the very least, better than any other living human being. If someone missed my latest example of perfection, I was sure to point it out.

Sometimes I actually failed to reach the impossible or complete the improbable. As the years went by, I attempted less and less. Because I was involved in an unhealthy relationship, I frequently heard about my lack of living skills and inability to cope. Crazy thinking, actions, and reactions were the norm.

*I didn't have to be God anymore. I didn't have to do things perfectly.*

Fortunately, my Higher Power steered me to OA, acceptance, and sanity. It somehow made sense to let God be God. I didn't have to be God anymore. I didn't have to do things perfectly. "Let go and let God" is a slogan of freedom for me. By using it, I have given myself permission to be human.

I now experience the joy of success and the knowledge that failure is simply one way that doesn't work. I'm free to try again. This slogan helps me keep my nose out of other people's inventories, so they can experience their own successes and failures.

Thanks, Higher Power, OA, and all my friends in the program.

— *Arizona USA*

# Learning Trust

When I first came to OA, I believed my life was in order. I felt happy with my food; I just wasn't happy with my weight. I had everything else under control, except that I didn't drive. I rarely had an unpleasant feeling. As soon as I became the least bit uncomfortable, I pulled food around me like a blanket. I was happy, happy, happy. The only other emotion I could express was rage. I lived like a baby, in a fantasy state, while trying to run my family's lives. The first lesson I learned in OA (after admitting I was a compulsive eater) was that I had no power over my loved ones' lives and that I was responsible only for making choices about my own life.

Although I came to OA with faith in a loving God, it took me years to put my trust in that God. Food finally drove me to the point where I knew that if I didn't fully surrender, all was lost. I mark my recovery from that day in October 1978 when I stood at the bottom and totally "let go and let God."

Today I know that God has given me the twin gifts of abstinence and sanity, and that my responsibility is to open my heart and mind to the Steps of this program. My daily choice is whether or not I will accept those gifts.

Almost without fail, I start my day with Step Eleven, which directs me to improve my conscious contact with God, as I understand God, through prayer and meditation. Throughout the day, I attempt to practice the principles of my program in all my affairs, carrying the OA message by example rather than coercion.

I am deeply grateful for the places I can go to hear OA spoken by my fellow recovering compulsive eaters around the world. Thank you all for being there for me and with me.

— *Anonymous*

# Looking in All the Wrong Places

When I first came to OA, I heard that it was a Twelve-Step program and recovery depended upon a power greater than myself. Many people mentioned God. I knew there had to be a catch. I had searched for God my whole life and never found him. If God was the source of recovery, and I couldn't find him, then this program would never work for me.

Then I went to my first Big Book study, and I found my God on page 55 of that book: "Actually we were fooling ourselves, for deep down in every man, woman, and child, is the fundamental idea of God" (*Alcoholics Anonymous*, 4th ed.). It goes on to say, "He was as much a fact as we were. We found the Great Reality deep down within us." God was inside me! No wonder I could never find him; I was looking outside myself. From that day on, my relationship with God has grown stronger with each passing day.

> *My concept of God as "man" was limiting, but a brilliant, white, loving light could be anywhere and do anything.*

I also had to change my concept of God. If he was inside me, he couldn't be the "man" I always thought he was. He had to go from being something tangible to being love, light, and energy. My concept of God as "man" was limiting, but a brilliant, white, loving light could be anywhere and do anything—even save me from my disease.

I went from believing that I was hopeless and would die from this disease to believing that my Higher Power can and will take me places beyond my wildest dreams. There is no limit to what my God and I can do together.

Even in all this glory, there is a catch. I have to step aside, be a "retired Higher Power," and let God be in charge of my life. Some days I still think, "I'm in control; I can do this." I have a rotten day until I realize I'm doing God's job, and I'm not doing it well. My Higher Power quietly and lovingly reminds me that I'm not God, and I turn things over. It's that simple.

Why do I complicate things? Why do I need to be continually shown that I can't do this alone? I think it's because my disease does not want me to recover. My disease blocks me from my Higher Power and tries to tell me that I'm in control, I know what's best for me, and I know what to do.

Every morning, before my feet even hit the floor, I paraphrase the first three Steps: "I can't do this, God. I know you can, and today I'll let you!" The difference even that much recovery makes in my life is amazing.

For today, I'm grateful that I've found "the source," and I can have recovery if I only let God do God's job.

— *Iowa USA*

# Who's Driving the Bus?

Step One prepared me for Step Two. I admitted my powerlessness and the unmanageability of my life. Then I came to believe that a power greater than myself could restore me to sanity. I had admitted to powerlessness; now I had to admit my insanity. I understand that this can be a stumbling block for many people. I was fortunate in being able to accept it without hesitation. I could recognize myself instantly in the crazy pedestrian of the Big Book, who repeatedly walked into traffic and suffered terrible injuries, only to step out again, surprised when the result was the same.

I had a history of using food inappropriately. We laugh at the old-time peddlers traveling from town to town selling the magic potion, the cure for every ailment. Food was my potion. I used it to subdue pain, to ease tension, to dull emotions, and to ease loneliness. Food was my best friend.

I continued to use it even after I recognized the terrible price it demanded. It provided short-term relief from distress only to leave me deeper in despair. Food is part of celebrating in our culture, but when abused as I abused it, it robbed me of the happy times, too. I could not sit still with any emotion. When I was stuffed full of food to the point of physical pain, I still turned to food for relief—driven by a compulsion over which I had no control.

When I found OA, admitting my insanity was a relief. The power greater than myself was the sticking point. I didn't open my mind to this for a long time. I had to recognize that ego and intellect are not firm foundations. They are steel barriers that cut me off from life. I had to end the debate. I had to become willing to suspend my unbelief and take a blind leap of faith. This was the key for me. This is the Step, according to Bill W., where we find the first promise of the program—the promise that we can be restored to sanity.

The remaining Steps outline what we must do to let the miracle unfold. A Higher Power can restore my sanity. To me, sanity means having food in its proper place as nourishment for my body. It means emerging from the food fog to live in the clarity of the moment. It means accepting good days and bad, pain and uncertainty, as well as exuberance, joy, and serenity. It means coming out of isolation to help others and to ask for help. It means resigning from my job as God. It means living the Steps as well as I can and recognizing that my Higher Power is always there for me.

Years ago, I came across a wonderful analogy. If you are on a bus that is speeding wildly down the road, totally out of control, it's time to open the driver's compartment to see what idiot is driving the bus. This question must remain front and center in my thinking: who is driving my bus today?

— *Nova Scotia, Canada*

# Sounds Like a Plan!

I can't think of a better time to talk about a plan of eating than before the holidays, some of my favorite times to binge. Before abstinence, my plan was to eat as much of my favorite binge foods as often as I could. I was miserable afterward.

I have a new plan now, one that God showed me eight years ago. The plan is more than just giving up binge foods, although that's part of it. In the beginning, this plan frightened me because it was a new way of eating. Instead of eating "everything that moved," God and I honestly looked at the foods and behaviors that were a problem for me and developed a plan I could follow one day at a time.

Give up junk food? I don't think so. Give up eating every time I feel the urge? I don't think so. Give up being miserable and fat? I don't think … really, God? Live one day at a time with a food plan that we have chosen together? I think I can do that. Give up the foods and behaviors that are slowly and surely killing me, one day at a time? Now that sounds like a plan!

God and I started this plan on January 1, 1992, the day my new life began. I committed to my Higher Power that I would live within the guidelines he put before me. God and I have agreed that if I put down the food, he will keep me out of it. God has more than come through for me all these years! It is God's miracle that the foods I once lived for are now just a fond and horrible memory. He helps me see that this new plan is a better way of life.

Some of you may want to know what my plan is, but that doesn't matter. My plan with God may not be your plan with God. I invite you to talk to your Higher Power and figure out a plan for you. Trust him, work the Twelve Steps, and recover from compulsive eating one day at a time. It works!

As the old adage says, "If we fail to plan, we plan to fail." Talk to your Higher Power; see what plans he has for you; and be happy, joyous, and free from compulsive eating.

— *Iowa USA*

# Following God

I was on my way to chair an OA meeting the other day, feeling anxious as I usually do in that situation. I was also anxious about being late, even though I had allowed ample time for my short trip. I thought I would have peace of mind if I managed the meeting setup perfectly. Old habits die hard.

Just as I started to speed up, a large truck turned in front of me. It seemed to take up the entire road. I could barely see where I was going. Worse yet, the truck and I were headed toward the same part of town. Each time I needed to turn, the truck turned just ahead of me. The traffic situation made passing impossible. I had no choice but to fall back and follow its lead. We arrived at the meeting location after a few minutes. The truck went on while I turned off, reaching the meeting with time to spare.

> *If I start mapping out each turn in advance, I'm going to hit a pothole or miss a turn and wind up in a dark alley wondering where I went wrong.*

Reflecting on this, I remembered how God leads me in life. He expects me to follow him blindly to a destination of peace and joy that I know is certain, but along a route only he knows. If I follow willingly, concentrating on the pavement directly ahead rather than on the next turn, God will lead me to the place I need to be each day. On the other hand, if I start mapping out each turn in advance, I'm going to hit a pothole or miss a turn and wind up in a dark alley wondering where I went wrong.

I am grateful to have found others in OA who are willing to help me let go of trying to control where my life is going. They encourage me to fix my eyes on the path that God has lain before me.

— *Texas USA*

## Surrender Brings Peace

I'm getting out of bed every morning and going to an unfulfilling job. I'm not in a relationship because the bad boys I attract stomp on my heart. My friends get on my nerves and disagree with me. My crazy family drives me insane every time I see them. I have no idea what I want to do with my life. I don't know where to turn, so I pray. I pray for the perfect job, the perfect man, the perfect friends, the perfect family, the perfect life. After all this praying, why do I still have no direction?

*After all this praying, why do I still have no direction?*

The above paragraph describes me in the twenty-nine years before I found Overeaters Anonymous. It describes the vicious cycle of self-destruction and hopelessness that was my life. It describes a compulsive overeater at her worst—blaming everyone and everything around her for her problems and hating God because he's not helping. It describes a person who is not willing to take responsibility for her life. It describes a person who is not willing to "let go and let God."

Through the OA rooms, through conversations with my sponsor and other OA members, and through surrendering, I have discovered an amazing thing: peace. Peace comes naturally with surrender. After giving up control of my food plan and following the direction of my sponsor for the last several months, I know in my heart that the right things will come for me. I'm not sure why I suddenly know that and trust it; I just do. I feel that God has lifted a weight from my shoulders, and now I can live every day under his plan instead of mine. This is good because I never had a plan that didn't include my binge foods.

Today, I get out of bed every morning and talk to my sponsor before going to an unfulfilling job. Today, I don't worry about being in a relationship because I know that I'm enough on my own. Today, I treat my friends with respect, as they do me. Today, I realize that my family is as sick as I am, and we need to be kinder to one another. Today, I have no idea what I want to do with my life, but I don't feel lost because of it. Today, I pray for God's will to shine on my path. Today, I pray for direction. Today, I pray for peace. Today, I ask God what he wants for me; then I wait and keep my eyes open to his suggestions.

Today, I am free because I have surrendered.

— *Pennsylvania USA*

## It Will Be Okay

Yesterday morning my husband told me he no longer loves me. Shattered, terrified, furious, and grief stricken, I wanted to scream and destroy furniture. I wanted someone to tell me that everything would be okay (as long as okay meant that things would turn out the way I wanted).

Recently, a sponsoree told me she was afraid her new boss wouldn't give her the usual holiday time off to spend with her family. I tried to tell her that even if she didn't get what she requested, she would be okay. What about her feelings of anger and resentment, she asked? I quoted these words from the Big Book that OA members have often quoted to me: "Unless I accept life on life's terms, I cannot be happy" (*Alcoholics Anonymous*, 3rd ed., p. 449). That acceptance didn't have to mean liking the situation; it meant being free of the need to fight its reality. It meant being open to the idea that we could be okay even if we didn't like the way things were.

As I reeled from the blow of my husband's revelation, I also saw the promises of OA being true in my life. I intuitively knew how to handle a baffling situation. I did not lash out at him, and I did not run away. Old ogres came up: my core terror of being abandoned;

the low self-esteem that tells me I'm unworthy of being loved; the magical thinking that said things had been going too well, so something bad had to follow. Yet, I did not have to act on any of it. I did not have to eat. I packed my lunch as usual. I made phone calls. I went to the home of a sponsoree who has a great deal of experience, strength, and hope to share in this area, and I went to a meeting that night.

I don't feel I am sailing through this perfectly. I can feel myself withdrawing and shutting down emotionally, an old habit from childhood. With abstinence and time spent practicing the OA program, I have the clarity to see this arise, accept it, and ask for help to know God's will to do the next right thing.

*I am in so much pain it feels as if I'm being burned alive. Nevertheless, I believe I can get through this.*

I hate not knowing what's going to happen. I am in so much pain it feels as if I'm being burned alive. Nevertheless, I believe I can get through this. God's will will not carry me where God's grace will not sustain me.

When I came into OA, I heard about a power that could relieve me of the desire to eat compulsively. This relief was unconditional; my abstinence would still work even if something bad happened to me. That has been true for almost eight years, and I am showing up again today with faith that care is available to me.

— *Massachusetts USA*

# Guideposts to God's Will

Often, it's difficult for me to know whether I'm in self-will when I make a decision or whether I'm following God's will. How am I learning to tell the difference? I know that it's more likely I'm following God's will if:

ᕯ I have participated with others and not isolated in making the decision.

ᕯ I have sought clarity from people whose programs I like and respect, such as my sponsor and long-term members.

ᕯ I have prayed about it.

ᕯ I have written in my journal about it.

ᕯ I have reached a decision and then "sat with it" for a bit instead of acting impulsively.

ᕯ I have a deep knowing in my heart and my gut, as well as having the knowledge in my brain.

ᕯ I view my decision as footwork, realizing that God may change the plan and that I must be flexible so I don't get tunnel vision.

ᕯ The decision enhances my life instead of being either detrimental or neutral. I can waste much of my life on neutral time fillers, such as reading or watching TV.

ᕯ I can accept others' suggestions and opinions about my decision, understanding the loving spirit in which they give their views, even if those views don't agree with mine. If I can accept their opinions without defensiveness, reflect on them, see what fits for me and what does not, and then make my decision, I'm more likely to have God's clarity.

These guideposts work for me in small decisions, such as whether to buy food on the way home from work (which generally is unsafe for me) or to go home and cook something. They also work for me in big decisions. Shall I change to part-time work or stay with full-time work? How can I best help a family member who is hurting without becoming a rescuer? I find that these specific guideposts help me. I hope they help you.

— *Pennsylvania USA*

# Threefold Stretching

Recovery is where you find it. Recently, I found it in the homily of a Sunday mass. The priest shared his enjoyment of running and the stretches he did to prevent injuries.

The instruction sheet for these stretches illustrated the body's position and direction to accomplish each stretch. It also described which muscles would be stretched and how the stretches worked. Few of us would know which muscles were being stretched without the instructions. I didn't and neither did the priest, but he trusted that those who wrote the instructions had more knowledge in the field.

Over the years, therapists have given me different stretches for backaches and pains in my legs caused by old injuries. When I do these stretches somewhat regularly, I have no pain in my back or legs, and the rest of my body feels vibrant and energized. I'm not talking about working out at a gym or exercising with equipment, but just stretching for a few minutes each day.

*Prayer is a form of spiritual stretching.*

The priest went on to suggest that prayer is a form of spiritual stretching. By putting our bodies and minds in certain positions and reaching, we begin to feel better. Our sense of spiritual well-being is proportional to our spiritual stretching.

This is when my Higher Power took the ball and ran with it. If I consider the Steps, Traditions, and tools of this program as simple stretches rather than as exercise or work, my life becomes a simple series of stretches from one stepping-stone to the next down the road of sane and happy usefulness.

I have learned in program that I'm not so much a slow learner as a fast forgetter. I wondered why this character defect was not swept away when I did my Sixth and Seventh Steps. Perhaps it is not a defect, but an asset improperly applied.

Each time I stretch, I forget a little of where I am stretching *from* and focus on where I am stretching *to*. Before OA, I reached for food whenever I faced a challenge. Since OA, I reach for a tool, a Step, or a Tradition. I've learned that they work much better, and I forget how I used to act.

The disease sneaks back occasionally, and I think I'll reach for the food. I have not been cured. I have received only a daily reprieve contingent on my working the Steps. How will my Higher Power know I want to walk with him if I don't have the opportunity to choose another path?

For today, I choose to live my life in the company of God and in the Fellowship of OA. Before program, I would get bent out of shape. In OA, I only have to stretch: physically, emotionally, and spiritually.

— *Alberta, Canada*

# Spiritual Connections

Recovery is threefold: physical, emotional, and spiritual. We've all heard about the three-legged stool and how we need all three legs to keep the stool from tipping over. It's odd how we come to Overeaters Anonymous because of our weight, but we stay for our sanity.

*I never imagined how much the concept of spirituality had to do with my physical recovery.*

I came into OA because I was fat, miserable, and hating myself. The other thing I came for was the "secret diet," but I found much more waiting for me. I never could have imagined how much the concept of spirituality had to do with my physical recovery.

I am not a member who was blessed with perfect recovery and perfect abstinence. I didn't work the Steps perfectly, nor was I perfectly willing to go to any length to recover. I did not work the Fourth Step for years, and when I did do it, it wasn't perfect.

We all recover in different ways, and each of us looks at our own recovery through different eyes. My recovery started with my emotions. I no longer thought I was stupid because I was fat. I found the courage to handle situations and to express my feelings and fears. I let go of my shame and hatred and felt more comfortable with myself. I lost hundreds of pounds between my ears, and that was a good feeling. Next, I slowly began losing weight, although I found no secret diets or magic pills. My Higher Power knew I needed to do this slowly so that I wouldn't think I didn't need this program anymore. My Higher Power knew I needed to keep coming back.

I didn't like it at the time and was often discouraged. Fortunately, I had a loving and supportive sponsor who modeled serenity and recovery, one day at time. I had great OA meetings and friends who loved me and encouraged me to keep coming back. I found a Higher Power whom I loved and who loved me.

Today I enjoy recovery on all three levels. Some days I am happy with where I am in my journey. Other days I am restless, irritable, and discontent. On these "growing days," I find my spiritual connection is lacking. To be happy, joyous, and free, I must stay in close personal contact with my Higher Power.

Some say physical recovery is the most important part of our journey, but I disagree. I became abstinent when I truly understood the words I was saying: "God, let me do your will today." Suddenly they were not just words; I was thinking what those words meant for me.

If I'm asking to do God's will, does that mean God would want me to eat too much, to stuff myself until I was miserable and uncomfortable? Does that mean God wants me to lie about what I ate or didn't eat that day? Does that mean God wants me to feel worthless, stupid, and miserable? I don't think so.

How can I be doing God's will when I am treating myself with disrespect? Does God want me to be impatient and controlling, or does God want me to serve others? Is my Higher Power loving and patient, and isn't that what is expected of me?

When I am not spiritually fit, I can expect my program and recovery to slip. The first thing that slips is my physical recovery. I gain weight and feel unhappy. The Big Book says on page 83, "The spiritual life is not a theory. We have to live it" (*Alcoholics Anonymous*, 4th ed.). Continual recovery means continual action. If I don't turn my day over to my Higher Power, I try to control my food and my life. The results are painful—not just to me, but to all those in my life.

I want physical recovery, so I will keep my connection with my Higher Power and continue the journey. If you are struggling with your abstinence or recovery, maybe it's time to take another look at your spiritual connections and see if you are willing to live the spiritual life we read about in the Big Book.

— *South Carolina USA*

# Discerning HP's Will

When I came to OA eleven years and 40 pounds (18 kg) ago, I had no spiritual life. During my time in program, I've slowly been building a relationship with a Higher Power. A few years ago, someone pointed out a paragraph on pages 97-98 of the OA "Twelve and Twelve" that has given me a simple and effective way of learning my Higher Power's will for me:

"There will be times when we're faced with an important decision and want to know our Higher Power's will. Our sponsor or OA friend might suggest that we pray about it, asking God to increase our desire to take the action if we're supposed to take it, or decrease our desire if we're not supposed to take it. After this prayer we stop worrying about making the decision right now, and we wait a day or so, meanwhile keeping our eyes, ears, and minds open. By the end of the waiting period we will inevitably find that we've gained a clearer perspective on the decision."

I do just as the book says. If I am worrying over whether to visit my mother during the holidays, I ask HP to increase or decrease my desire to take the trip, depending on which action is HP's will for me. Then comes the most important part: I have to wait. I am a compulsive and impulsive person, so waiting is hard for me. But I find waiting to be the most important part of the process. I usually experience a shift of feelings inside me, but sometimes I don't. Then I can ask again, or I can choose to believe that HP is leaving this one up to me. This is the only way I've found to bring my will into line with HP's will.

As an impulsive person, I wasn't always aware of when I was at a decision point. I raced through my decisions, doing what I felt like doing at the time. Early in program I asked HP to slow me down and show me where the decision points were. I couldn't ask for help with a decision unless I knew I was making one. I prayed for this and received the awareness I needed.

— *Anonymous*

# Beating the Hatred

I can't say enough about keeping a positive outlook on life. I start my day being grateful for another wonderful day. I thank God for what I have, and I don't worry about what I don't have. God gives me what I need each day, and I am grateful.

When I was young and overweight, I begged God to let me wake up skinny. I hated school because everyone made fun of me for being overweight. My thighs rubbed together and hurt after I walked to classes. I quit school at sixteen because of my weight. I made A's in all my classes except physical education. I couldn't keep up with the exercises and games because I was obese. The teacher failed me for not changing into my gym clothes, and I hated her. I was only about thirteen then and filled with hatred.

I sought the love and relief in food that I could not find in my life. I started dieting when I became three pounds heavier than my dad. I starved the weight off, worked as a waitress, and loved my life for a while.

> *I sought the love and relief in food that I could not find in my life.*

Because of the hate I still felt, I slowly started eating compulsively again. The weight came back with the births of my beautiful daughters. I continued to eat compulsively and was on one diet after another.

Through the Twelve Steps, a sponsor, friends, and working the OA program, I no longer feel the hatred. The people, places, and things around me look different today. I thank this program and my Higher Power for these changes. I am grateful to my best friend who brought me to these rooms and gave me the courage to find God. She is the angel God sent to bring me home to him.

Now I realize that God has always been guiding me. I know that I am loved, and I know that I love myself enough to work my program and share it with others. My life depends on working this program, and abstinence is the most important thing in my life. Without abstinence I would not have a close relationship with my Higher Power or have my positive outlook on life.

Thank you all for being part of my recovery. Without you sharing your experience, strength, and hope, the disease would take over my life. You are my lifeline to and from my Higher Power.

I can keep a positive attitude because I know God is taking care of the small things and I don't have to worry. Life is wonderful. I let go and let God do the impossible.

— *Anonymous*

# CHAPTER THREE

# A Spiritual Solution to Our Disease

*Developing a relationship with the Higher Power of
our understanding and working the Twelve Steps
pave the road to freedom from compulsive eating.*

# A Road Out of Insanity

I am a recovering food addict who works in the field of eating disorders. My Higher Power gently (and not so gently at times) embraced me and brought me to OA. I have always wondered why God chose me to recover because I've seen so many who didn't make it. I've come to the decision that God wanted me to help others.

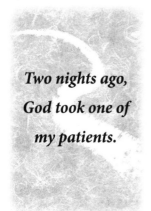

*Two nights ago, God took one of my patients.*

I have always known that this disease kills people. Two nights ago, God took one of my patients, a forty-seven-year-old man who weighed 490 pounds (223 kg). The doctors said he died of heart failure, but in my eyes he died of compulsive overeating. I experienced so many feelings: anger at God, shock, disbelief, and intense grief and pain.

I came home from my OA meeting tonight, picked up my new *Lifeline*, and decided to write this. My motive, in part, is to beg anyone out there who has this deadly disease to open his or her eyes, heart, soul, and mind. Don't wait until it's too late. Embrace the Twelve Steps and OA. There is hope, a different way, a road out of the insanity of food.

The other reason I am writing is to help myself process my anger at this deadly disease. My sponsor helped me make sense of my patient's death tonight. She said to me, "At least he died with hope; he knew there was a different way." That way is OA, the Twelve Steps, and God. May you find him now.

— *Texas USA*

# Physical Problem, Spiritual Solution

A wealth of eating-disorder-related stories have been featured lately in newspapers and magazines, on the radio and TV. A wide variety of suggestions have been offered as solutions for binge eating, anorexia, and bulimia. Most involve behavior modification: simply push yourself away from the table when you're full. Others recommend self-knowledge: now that you realize your faulty relationship with food, you can stop this destructive behavior.

In theory, these approaches should work. In reality, a food addict like me cannot stop by using a thought process or psychological evaluation! Over twelve years of recovery have taught me that to stop my physical problem of out-of-control bingeing, I need a spiritual solution.

The physical problem manifested itself as a craving for food—day and night—that was beyond my power to control. The insane urge to stuff my body with food, to fill up some unidentifiable empty space, drove me to act in ways I can barely recall without cringing.

Digging into frozen or burned food. Retrieving food from the trash can. Isolating in front of the television with the curtains closed and the phone left for the answering machine. Buying bigger and bigger clothes. Turning down social invitations due to a preoccupation with food and body fat. The list is long and filled with embarrassment.

I came to OA looking for physical relief. I longed for a slender body and a sane relationship with food. I have been given both. My path has been clearly defined by three moderate and balanced meals per day—free of second helpings, snacks, or binge foods. I see the first bite beyond this prescription as a way to reactivate the eating disorder. I avoid it at all costs.

To access the power I need to stay on course, I have had to turn to the Steps of our program. I don't have the necessary power to adhere to an eating plan any more than I can stick to a diet. The solution has been to turn to a Higher Power, a power beyond my limitations.

With every fiber of my being, I believe in and count on the help of this power to keep me safe from that first compulsive bite. To be sure, I do my footwork: meetings, reading, phone calls, writing, and the study and use of the Twelve Steps. Through this effort on my part, coupled with the honest desire to stay in recovery, my Higher Power walks me through my everyday life—safe from the disease that was ravaging my body and soul.

Beyond the physical recovery of abstinence and a slender, healthy body, I've been given the tools and power to build my new life. I have a darling husband, a wealth of friends, a fascinating career, travels filled with wonder, and a deep sense of satisfaction in daily living.

I imagine that the news features about eating disorders and their numerous solutions are of value to some people. I'm not one of them. I seem most suited to the Twelve-Step program. Today I'm living beyond my wildest and most heartfelt dreams. These facts are proof that OA works.

— *California USA*

## The OA Door

*The pain it took to get me here engulfed my very soul.*
*The food I bought, consumed, and wore had never made me full,*
*Yet through the day and nighttime too the food screamed out my name.*
*My efforts to resist its pull were short-lived and in vain.*

*"Oh, God," I cried, "If you're there at all, please rescue me and soon."*
*I sat alone on the edge of death in the fullness of the moon.*

*Rhapsodies floated through my mind; their tunes I could not hear.*
*All of life was drummed away by constant hopeless fear.*
*Afraid to peek within myself, I wallowed in my grief;*
*The trip inside was painful and usually only brief.*

*"Oh, God," I cried, "If you're there at all, please rescue me and soon."*
*I sat alone on the edge of death in the fullness of the moon.*

*Darkness overwhelmed me; I was sickened to the core,*
*When at last a gentle guide brought me to this door.*
*I could not see this guide of mine, I only heard him say,*
*"Go in, my child, and you'll be filled; there is no other way."*

*"Oh, God," I cried, "If you're there at all, please rescue me and soon."*
*I sat alone on the edge of death in the fullness of the moon.*

*A healing love enveloped me and made me yearn for more.*
*I trembled as they shared their hope; my heart began to soar.*
*These strangers preached a message that I had never heard;*
*I followed in their footsteps believing in their word.*

*"Oh God," I cried, "Now I know you're there, you've been there all along.*
*You led me to recovery's door. You've taught me to be strong."*

*No longer do I sit alone and dwell with grief and pain.*
*The strangers have become my friends; they helped me to be sane;*
*They accept my limitations; they applaud my progress too.*
*Most importantly, they showed me how, to my own self to be true.*

*"Oh God," I cried, "Now I know you're there, you've been there all along.*
*You led me to recovery's door. You've taught me to be strong."*

*— Arizona USA*

# The Inside Track

One symptom of this disease is that we seek an external solution, when the real solution comes from within. The outward methods I used to tackle the disease of compulsive overeating never had any permanence. At best, the methods were a temporary fix. The diets, therapies, and medications just stopped working for me. Confusion and frustration set in. No, there was no human solution.

Ultimately, I came to know that the answer I seek is truly the inner spirit—the spirit of God within me. The Twelve Steps tackle the job of clearing away the debris, a cleansing process that brings me closer to a fulfilling union with the spirit within. There is no external answer, just the internal one.

*If the disease of compulsive overeating brings us together, our recovery keeps us together.*

Each day, I remain open to the nurturing of that answer. Part of my daily prayer is that I may overcome any human frailty that blocks the internal answer. I stumble and fumble, impeding my own progress, but I can learn from this. Faith grows. Hope increases. New meaning comes to life.

If the disease of compulsive overeating brings us together, our recovery keeps us together. Together, as we move closer to the cell door to gain freedom, we notice that the key to the door is on the inside. God's light illumines the way out for us. The inside track is our salvation; we are never alone.

— *Ohio USA*

# Answers Sought, Prayers Delivered

No matter how long I'm abstinent, I find that abstinence requires constant vigilance. One Saturday, I experienced what I would describe as a "Kodak moment."

I began my day as usual, spending half an hour praying to God for abstinence. I called my sponsorees and sponsor; had a candlelit, abstinent breakfast; exercised at the gym; attended two of my favorite meetings, sharing and giving service—all before noon. After the meetings, I had a two-hour lunch with a sponsoree, sharing and doing the Twelve Steps.

After running errands, I went to see an OA friend and spent six hours with his one-year-old son. The time with the boy was wonderful. I felt as though God were laying his hands directly on my heart. I've been trying to experience things I really love—being around children, watching sunrises and sunsets, writing stories, listening to music—because then I feel God's presence the most. Later, I had an abstinent dinner and thought the night was over. I couldn't have asked for a more perfect day—a "Kodak moment."

But when I got home, I was starving. I opened my roommate's cabinets where all his goodies were stored. I flipped through the telephone book to find restaurants that would deliver. I calculated how much money I could squeeze on my credit cards to binge—all the sick, food-obsessive thoughts we OA members experience before picking up that first bite.

Thank you, God. He entered my thoughts and came to my rescue, just as I had prayed for that morning. I regained sanity, reached out, and used the telephone tool to tell someone what was happening to me, but no one answered. I thought of the passage in "How It Works" in the Big Book (*Alcoholics Anonymous*, 4th ed., p. 58), which says that we must be "willing to go to any length," so I decided to use the writing tool. By writing down my feelings, I discovered what was troubling me. It was a happy day, but spending those hours with the boy made me long to be a husband, a father, a family man. Once I got in touch with these feelings, the cravings passed. I've discovered that often when I start craving, an uncomfortable feeling, good or bad, brews in me, and that causes the craving.

Thank you, God, for the Steps and the tools—for my willingness to go any length. The old me would have given up after the unanswered phone calls. The new me wants to work through these feelings. God willing, someday I will be a father and have the family I so desire; but if I choose to eat, I will lose everything and won't be able to experience the happy, joyous, and free life I am promised. That night, I got on my knees and thanked God for doing for me what I can never do for myself.

This program doesn't promise a life free of hard times or uncomfortable feelings. It does promise me a method of dealing with them through the Twelve Steps and the tools. Thank you, God, for another abstinent day!

— *Florida USA*

# CHAPTER FOUR

## Spiritual Experiences
## Before and During the Program

*God brought these individuals to OA—*
*and kept them there.*

# Miracle in Minneapolis

Not long ago, after ten years in program and three years of serious relapse, I scheduled a business trip to the midwestern United States. I would spend two days in Milwaukee, then fly to Minneapolis for two more days and then endure another lonely weekend in a strange hotel, avoiding the hotel mirrors, watching junk TV, and eating alone in my room.

The week went well. But before each appointment, even though I was certain most would go well, I would stop at a convenience store and buy a bag of sweets to see me through the day. I needed them, I convinced myself; after all, I was nervous. What's more, I had earned them. I was driving a rental car on strange roads and was frequently lost. If that wasn't suffering, what was?

I also knew there was a half-pound or more of similar items waiting for me back at the hotel. With any luck, I thought that by the time I returned to my room, the maintenance staff would have thoughtfully removed the mirrors, and I'd be able to eat undisturbed by any visible evidence of how obese I'd become.

I checked into the Minneapolis hotel late Wednesday night and ordered dinner from room service. Within half an hour, I was propped up comfortably in bed, watching TV and diving into my dessert. My finger paused on the remote control briefly as I flicked past the hotel's video event board; there was some sort of OA activity going on at the hotel.

"Hah!" I thought; I'd seen this before. The last time I tried going to a hotel meeting in a distant city, there was nobody there but me. Why try again? I finished my meal and went to sleep.

The next morning I woke, ordered breakfast from room service, showered, and turned on the TV. There was that OA stuff again! I decided that surely it had to be something local—or at best regional. Big deal, I thought: the last time I'd tried a hotel meeting ... I dressed and left for my appointments.

Toward the end of the day, I was driving back to the hotel feeling pleased with my work but consumed with self-loathing. Eating junk from my purse didn't help. I turned on the radio, thinking some music would make me feel better.

Suddenly I heard a pastor on the radio, imploring listeners to pray for deliverance from whatever held them in bondage. "All right, God," I offered. "I'll try it. Please ... I've asked you before. I've asked for the willingness. I'm driving on a strange highway in a strange car and feeling very silly, but I'll ask you again: please release me from the bondage of food!"

As I entered the hotel, I planned my evening my way: I would go to my room, order dinner from room service, and perhaps check out OA later. But as I entered through an unfamiliar door, I found myself at the foot of the escalator leading to the OA events just one flight above. I let the loving, invisible hand at my back push me gently upstairs and over to the registration table, where I tearfully registered for what I discovered was OA's 1995 World Service Convention. I wrote a check and emptied the junk food from my purse into OA's wastebasket. Later, before bed, I unwrapped all remaining pieces of junk food and flushed them down the toilet.

The miracles did not end there. On Saturday morning I wandered aimlessly, looking for somewhere to be. Spotting another OA member, I struck up a conversation and followed her into an unmarked room. "Oops!" I thought. Then I discovered it was the gay and lesbian special-interest meeting. I was stunned. My three-year period of relapse appeared to have begun with the recognition, in therapy, of my bisexuality. I had suppressed all thoughts and actions on that subject and had hurt myself terribly in the process. In that circle, I heard my story told again and again and then told

*I unwrapped all remaining pieces of junk food and flushed them down the toilet.*

mine. It was okay. I was okay! There was nothing to fear here. I could embrace my deepest fears and begin to heal.

As I left Sunday morning to catch my flight home, I discovered a baby bird resting in the sunshine on one of the hotel paths. I approached with care, speaking softly, musically. Stooping, I offered her my index finger and invited her to hop on, to join me in welcoming this extraordinary day.

She paused, looked me squarely in the eye, issued a ceremonial poop, and flew off. Her motion through the air was that gently comic flight common to baby birds and to someone newly abstinent in OA: up and down she went. Would she make it? I wondered. I chose to believe she would.

Settling in the area of low bushes across the parking lot, she did. And I knew that through the grace of my Higher Power and the loving Fellowship of OA, I could make it too—one day at a time, in this program that has already given me so much.

— *New Hampshire USA*


# No Cuddles in the Cupboard

I was recently brought both to my knees and my senses by a loving Higher Power, this time manifesting himself through my three-year-old son.

Three years before my son was born, someone gave me a phone number for OA. I firmly believe that God didn't deem me ready to "come home" until the arrival of Sam, so that his developing, tender years could break through my stubborn and resentful exterior. I also believe that God uses my son when, for whatever reason, I cannot tune in to him, and I need a firm nudge for my recovery.

Such a nudge hit me last week when the two of us were mooching around the house with not much to do. Sam had followed me into the kitchen, bored and looking for something to eat, or so I thought. He started to say, "Mummy, I think I'll have…"

I should explain here that I assume he's having a growth spurt, because he seems to be continually eating. I automatically turned towards the cupboard to reach for some goodies, when he finished his sentence with "… a cuddle."

I stopped sharply, but God wasn't finished with me yet. I decided to tease him, opening the cupboard doors and then the 'fridge, all the while saying, "No, can't see one in here."

Sam fell about laughing, saying, "You don't find kisses and cuddles in cupboards, do you, Mummy?"

I knelt down to him and scooped him towards me, crying and laughing at the same time, and said, "No darling, you don't, but Mummy does."

*"You don't find kisses and cuddles in cupboards, do you, Mummy?"*

I can't honestly remember whether I continued to overeat that day or not. What I do know is that several days later, after much earnest praying and reading, I am experiencing my second day of abstinence. This is my second experience of my compulsion being lifted in the seven months since I found OA. I took Step Three again that day and began to understand the difference between surrender and submission. Surrender gives me hope, and the promise that the door I've been banging my head against for so many years will one day open wide, so I can not only see the sunlight but actually go through and bask in its glory.

I thank God for my son, and I thank God for OA.

— *Hampshire, England*

# Justifiable Anger?

"It is a spiritual axiom that every time we are disturbed, no matter what the cause, there is something wrong with us. If somebody hurts us and we are sore, we are in the wrong also." I was stunned the first time I read this in the AA "Twelve and Twelve" (*Twelve Steps and Twelve Traditions*, p. 90). Bill W. goes on to ask, "What about 'justifiable' anger?" Of course for us compulsive eaters, all our anger is justified, or so we think, because we know for sure other people are crazy and everything is all their fault. However, the "Twelve and Twelve" goes on to say, "We have found that justified anger ought to be left to those better qualified to handle it."

Recently, I had the opportunity to deal with what I thought was justifiable anger. A contractor who reports to me at work forwarded an email message to me by mistake. In it he referred to me, saying, "This employee, in an uncharacteristic burst of efficiency, actually replied in a timely way to my inquiry." When I read it, I felt hurt, angry, and as though I had been kicked in the stomach. How dare he say this about me, and especially in such a hostile and sarcastic way?

In the past, I would have cried all night, felt like a failure, never told a soul about it, and carried these bad feelings with me to my grave. Instead, I called an OA friend and read the message to her. When I read it aloud, it didn't sound quite as bad as it had on my first reading. She suggested I write about it, which I did. What came out was that there was some truth in what he had said. This was painful to accept. Sometimes I've had to wait for a reply from my superiors, and so my tardiness has not been my fault. But just as often, I've been too busy to find the information a coworker needed, so I let the request for help go, hoping he or she would forget about it.

I called another OA member and read her what I had written. I didn't know if the contractor realized he had forwarded me the memo, but two days later I had to meet with him. To his credit, he brought it up. He said, "I sent you a memo by mistake," and he quoted what he had written. I said, "I guess it could have been much worse." He said, "I'm sorry this happened." I looked him in the eye and said,

"I needed to read what you wrote." He said, "I know it's often not your fault and you have to wait for guidance from your superior." I acknowledged that was often true. Just like that, it was over.

But not quite. Right there in the man's office, I had what I can only describe as an intensely spiritual experience. I felt the presence of God, enveloped and safe, loving and loved, at peace and serene. The man was still speaking to me, but his words seemed to be coming from a long distance away, and I could barely hear them. It probably only lasted five seconds, but its effects lasted much longer.

*Right there in the man's office, I had what I can only describe as an intensely spiritual experience.*

As a compulsive overeater and former failure in Life 101, I can't afford anger, justified or not. I must follow the Twelve Steps, writing my feelings down on paper and reading them to a trusted person, acknowledging my part in situations, becoming ready to have my character defects removed, and asking my Higher Power to remove those character defects. Then I decide whether I need to make amends to anyone, and I make them, usually by changing my behavior. (You can bet that now I'm trying to respond to that contractor in a timelier manner!) Recovery is a process, a sane way of living, and it works in any situation, but especially with anger.

Recently I heard on the radio, "If I'm not the problem, there is no solution." To me this is another way of saying the Serenity Prayer. Today I believe I can change only my own attitudes, my own behaviors, and the situations I create. This meant leaving an abusive relationship when I finally realized I couldn't change the other person and was tired of blaming him for my unhappiness.

So the next time you're disturbed, whatever the cause, try working the Twelve Steps. They work if you work them!

— *Anonymous*

# CHAPTER FIVE

# Connecting with Higher Power

*Prayer and meditation yield gratitude and serenity,*
*the gifts of the program.*

# A Letter from God

I take the Eleventh Step and my spirituality seriously, so I have a running dialogue with my Higher Power throughout the day.

One morning at an OA retreat, I had been asked to do the service of leading morning meditation. I wrote exactly what I needed at the time. Here it is:

My Dear Child,

I know you have issues with trust, and it's often difficult for you to believe in me. So it may seem hard for you to accept my unconditional love and the idea that I am indeed concerned with every aspect of your life.

You are in this place because I brought you here. Be open to what I have to tell you, show you, and give you.

Your disease helped you cope with life before. It made it tolerable, but now it's time to let go of the ways of the past. I have such big plans for you! Trust that these plans are good. I did not bring you this far to let you fall. You are at the edge of the cliff, and I keep calling to you to step off. You shout, "I'll fall!" but I'm telling you, you'll fly and soar like an eagle.

You are stronger than you know. I will empower you if you ask me. I will help you make all the difficult decisions and keep the commitments. I will put people in your life to help you. I will never allow you to be tempted beyond your ability to resist, or even ask anything of you that I have not already empowered you to do.

Those inner yearnings you have are also my desires for you: peace, love, and recovery. I want you to have all of them.

Love, Your Higher Power

— *Illinois USA*

# Give It Time

It's important to me to take the time to sit back and open myself to what would best link me with my Higher Power. Sometimes it's a prayer-book reading. Sometimes I just sit and let images emerge. Other times a word or phrase pops up for me to explore in my journal. Sometimes I need to read a Step or Tradition.

But I have to give it time. When I first started scheduling time for morning prayer and meditation, I was amazed at the serenity I received. I began to realize that this HP had real power in my life. This morning meditation helped me shed the compulsive plans and worries that arose as I anticipated my day. Over time, I was better able to let God's guidance and power flow through me throughout the whole day. It was like having a strategy and pep talk from a supportive coach who believed in me.

I must admit, though, that I also have days when it's almost impossible just to sit and be open. My instinct tells me to flee. But I know better things await me if I stay.

The discipline of regular prayer and meditation is vital for my daily health. I've learned techniques from many sources. One author saw herself as a simple wooden flute, hollowed out and full of holes. By emptying herself and becoming receptive to the breath of God, she would sing God's song throughout her day.

I gain purpose and direction from the analogy of serving as an instrument of God's song. Since I began my recovery, I see that the challenge is to let go of control. When I want to be in charge, or feel I have to be, my throat tightens up and the whole song is forced and choppy. This is why I need to surrender control to my Higher Power every day. I want my prayer and meditation to be a time to invite God's melody to sing through me.

— *Nebraska USA*

# My Step-Three Prayer

One evening I wrote all the reasons why I felt I couldn't take Step Three. I had been agonizing over this Step because I didn't see my Higher Power in the same way as other people whose stories I'd read or heard.

I believe that our abilities to think, reason, and make choices are part of God's gifts. To turn my life over to God, or even to do God's will, seemed to say that I had to refuse my innate gifts. I have always believed in a God that watches what we do and can guide us in making correct choices. He is there to lean on for strength or to ask for guidance. But I never have and cannot believe in a God who would send a punishment if I "disobeyed" his word.

A God I fear isn't one I can love. I could never love anything or anyone that I was afraid of. After reading many books about religion, I realized that my views were not that different from some religious theology and ideology. I was reassured by that knowledge. I knew I was not just manufacturing a Higher Power that would suit me so I wouldn't have to work the program. I realized that I had to work the program to suit my idea of a Higher Power or God.

*How can I turn my life or will over to someone I don't think is there to receive it?*

But the problem arose, "How can I turn my life or will over to someone I don't think is there to receive it?" I don't believe that God is there to solve my problems for me. I don't believe that he sits upon some heavenly throne casting out rewards to those who seek, and plagues and tragedies to those who stray, causing events to happen or not happen at his discretion. I've always believed that human beings had some say in choosing the course their lives would take. So how could I give my life to someone I believed was there to guide, but not to control?

Trying to work the program to the best of my ability, I prayed about it. I wrote about all my worries, fears, and doubts. I read in my literature that the most important thing about taking Step Three is that I want to; I wanted to very much, but I had just listed a whole slew of reasons why I could not. When I read what I had written, I began to realize that if I took out every "can't" from my sentences, I would have written a lot of reasons why I can. So I did.

I took the negativity out of those statements and rewrote them as a prayer. The prayer both asks for those things that are in his power to give and reminds me that I must also take action and be responsible. I call this "My Step-Three Prayer." I say it every morning and every night.

One of the lines in "My Step-Three Prayer" reminds me not to act on impulse, but to take time out and ask for guidance to do the right thing. "Time out" has become one of my personal slogans that I use during the course of the day to remind me of my program. God's will, to me, is simply stated in the phrase, "Do the right thing." I know that God won't punish me if I don't do his will, but chances are that I'll bring a punishment upon myself for not making a positive choice. Taking time out to step back from a situation allows me to seek his strength to handle it in the best way. When I make wise choices, I find serenity.

I've also found, since spending more time with my Higher Power and seeking his knowledge, that amazing little coincidences have happened. I say "coincidences" because I still can't believe there is someone planning my life for me, causing the course of events to happen in a way that will benefit me, if only I ask. I don't like to think that my life or others' lives have been ordained simply because I chose to ask for something I needed. My Higher Power isn't orchestrating the world to suit me; he's orchestrating me to suit the world.

After much spiritual reading, I am coming to understand my own interpretation of prayer and what it means to me. Before OA, I spent my days seeing negativity and then eating so I wouldn't have to experience it. Since I've started making prayer a habit, I don't see so much negativity. Often, when I have a problem, I pray about it, meditate a few moments, and then let it go. Within a few days, quite often, some answer will come when I least expect it, when my mind wasn't even agonizing over the problem. It has been written that these situations or "coincidences" have always happened, but most of us have been blind to them. Prayer opens my eyes. It allows me to see the good things that are already here, if I will only seek them out.

I personally think that prayer opens communication between the heart and the mind, getting our hearts and minds focused in the same direction. How many times have I said, or heard others say, "My mind knows what I should do, but I just can't convince my heart"?

At those times, I become utterly confused and find myself being torn in opposite directions. Bringing my spiritual self into the picture provides a mediator. When I communicate my problems to my Higher Power, I become honest and aware of what I'm truly feeling and thinking. Soon an answer comes that serves to unite the heart and mind. And since a united front is stronger than a divided one, I also gain the strength to carry out the solution.

— *Florida USA*


## Six Little Words

I sat over coffee after a meeting, looking as miserable as I felt. I was deep in self-pity and resentment. After several wonderful months of "pink cloud" recovery, my bubble had burst with the news of a friend's terminal illness. It was so unfair. How could God let this happen, on top of my other problems? My sponsor approached and asked what was wrong.

"I'm angry with my Higher Power," I blurted out.

"Did you pray about it?"

Obviously, she had not heard properly. "It's my Higher Power that I'm angry with. How can I pray about that?"

"You need to pray about it."

I looked at her in amazement. Clearly, the woman had learned nothing from her eighteen years in OA. "Poor thing," I thought, "she's losing it." I began, with carefully chosen words, as if talking to a child, to explain my pain and anger. The words came faster and faster as I poured out my heart, trying to help her see that my problems were more complicated than she could understand.

*I was actually having an honest, no-holds-barred conversation with God.*

When I finally stopped, exhausted but sure that now I would hear the words of wisdom I had come to expect from her, she said: "You need to pray about it."

I sat back, shocked and disappointed. She had not heard a word I'd said. She had always been so helpful before. Why wasn't she getting it? She made me promise to pray and I did, just to get away from her. But I did not mean it.

I went home, still angry, and went to bed. All I could hear in my head was, "You need to pray about it," and it made me even more rebellious. This program was useless! Why did I ever think it would work? Finally, I said out loud: "All right! I'll do what I promised— just to prove to you that it doesn't work."

And I did. Grudgingly, at first, then with more openness, I told my Higher Power exactly why I was so angry with him.

In addition, I mentioned why I could not trust him. Suddenly I realized that, for the very first time, I was actually having an honest, no-holds-barred conversation with God. I had been the one keeping that door closed, not my Higher Power. There came over me a sudden understanding that God was not there to prevent me from feeling pain but to help me face it, and I felt both deeply humbled and comforted at the same time. I was no longer struggling alone.

After my emotional torrent of complaints, my sponsor had listened and helped me with just six little words. I guess my sponsor had learned a thing or two, after all!

— *Ontario Canada*


## Spiritual Growth as I See It

Spiritual growth doesn't happen overnight. The key word is growth. Growth takes time. A seed is a perfect example. First it has to be planted in fertile soil. It must be kept warm and moist. In time it will sprout and take root. Each day it feeds on the water and sun until a stem emerges from underneath the soil. It continues to feed daily, as the stem grows and leaves form. In time it gets bigger and bigger, and then one day it forms buds. The buds blossom into beautiful, soft, colorful petals. The petals form the flower. The seed could not have grown into a flower by itself. It needed to be planted and nourished daily with moisture and sunlight, and it needed time to grow. Without continual moisture and sun it would have wilted, withered, dried up, and blown away.

I am the same way. I cannot grow spiritually by myself. A seed had to be planted in my heart, and for that seed to grow, it had to be nourished daily with prayer, devotion, and meditation. To grow closer to my Higher Power, I need to feed on his word. To do this I must have a commitment to God and myself, because I cannot do it on my own strength.

I can do this every day by being honest with myself, admitting that I'm powerless, and I need God's strength and courage. I must be open-minded so I don't draw conclusions before considering all options. I must be willing to make changes, to follow God's will, and to trust that he knows what is best for me.

If I feed myself every day, I will grow spiritually just like the flower. In time, I will blossom into a beautiful, soft, colorful person. If I don't feed myself daily, I will wilt, wither, dry up, and blow away, just like the flower.

— *Massachusetts USA*

# God, Me, and the VCR

Steps Ten, Eleven, and Twelve are often called the daily living Steps, because here we practice daily what we've been doing in the first nine Steps.

The continuing inventory is important so we don't sink back into our old, addictive thinking. Admitting wrongs helps to clean up the messes we make when they're still easy to clean up.

There are several different kinds of Tenth Steps, ranging from a quick, spot check (What's going on here?) to an inventory as searching as a Fourth Step.

At the end of the day I imagine that I'm in a comfortable armchair talking with my HP. Together we watch a fast-forward replay of the day on the VCR. Then I ask myself, "Where am I physically, emotionally, and spiritually? Physically, was my food as clean as I would like, or was I playing games with my food plan, such as selecting the biggest apple ever seen and calling it one apple? Did I get enough rest and exercise? Emotionally, what did I feel? Was I angry, upset, or otherwise disturbed? Is there anything for which I owe amends?"

*I imagine that I'm in a comfortable armchair talking with my HP.*

Spiritually, I ask, "Did I do my prayer and meditation and continue to reach out toward God?" Since my OA program is an important part of my spiritual development, I also review how I'm working the tools of the program.

"Where am I with respect to abstinence (a plan of eating), OA meetings, phone calls, service, sponsorship, literature, writing, and anonymity? Do I need to practice any of these tools?" I've noticed that most of the people who are struggling with their OA program are not working one or more of these eight tools, so I find it useful to review the list. Of course, being human, I sometimes fall asleep before I finish.

— *Anonymous*

## Talking to HP

When I had lost all faith in myself, the OA program, the world, and even God, I kept on talking with my HP. I kept on talking because I didn't want to lose the life I had earned and been given in program. This continual talking has worked from the beginning of my program, so even when I believe my HP does not exist, I continue talking to him.

*Even when I believe my HP does not exist, I continue talking to him.*

I spoke to HP when I got up in the morning and fell in love with the way the sunlight illuminated the room, or when I saw the various birds dancing and fighting in the air with a grace that no man-made machine could possess. I saw the miracle of life in a patch of brilliantly colored flowers and thanked my HP. And when I was alone at night and believed I had no one to talk to, could not lift a pen or a book, and felt the black clouds of despair beginning to choke me, I shut my eyes and poured forth a string of heartfelt pleas to HP: please don't let me fall back into that black pit of compulsive bingeing and purging. I prayed for the strength to believe, even as I admitted my disbelief, and kept chanting inside my head, "I believe in the one who believes in me." I prayed until the pain and fear and craving left me.

As I progressed in program, I began to talk to HP as if he were my constant companion, thinking the best of me, supporting me, and telling me the painful truth in the most loving and constructive way for my growth and healing. HP spoke to me when I had a car accident on the way to a meeting (he kept me abstinent). HP spoke to me when I had two painful relationship breakups (he kept me abstinent). HP spoke to me when banks of black clouds smothered me with aching depression (he kept me abstinent).

I realize now that HP was always speaking to me, but I couldn't hear him until I began speaking with all my heart and willingness, even if the amount of willingness could not fill a thimble at that moment. However, as the promises of the program began coming true, along with the inevitable problems of daily living, I became too busy to speak to HP. Then I couldn't hear him until more pain drove me to more meetings and more sessions with him. And guess what! The burdens of life were easier to manage.

I don't follow this program perfectly. I don't have all the answers. I still have defects of character and pain in my life, but I also have a joy and contentment that were never open to me in my obsession. As long as I keep talking to my HP in whatever manner and with as much faith as possible, asking only for the strength to do his will for me, one day at a time I will hear him.

— *New York USA*

# Whose Will?

Lately I've been praying to my HP to show me what to do to take care of myself today and what to do as I approach another crossroad in life. I ask to know God's will and be graced with the power to carry it out. I've been praying that my will aligns with HP's will. When I let go and let God, I'm much more serene, and staying abstinent is not a struggle.

*What is my will, and what is God's will? Sometimes I'm confused.*

What is my will, and what is God's will? Sometimes I'm confused. During quiet time, I've focused on a passage from OA's "Twelve and Twelve." It suggests in Step Eleven that I ask God to increase the desire for something if it is God's will and decrease the desire if it is not. My past prayers were lists of what I wanted. I never thought that some desires were not good for me.

I've also meditated on a passage from page 559 of the Big Book: "We are taught to differentiate between our wants (which are never satisfied) and our needs (which are always provided for)" (*Alcoholics Anonymous*, 4th ed.). My disease is one of "not-enoughness." Before OA, nothing was ever enough. I was always waiting for something I wanted so I could be happy. Today, I usually have a sense of spiritual abundance and feel good in my skin. I am confident that God will fulfill my needs.

Some days I have the "I wants," and I pray and meditate on it. My Higher Power never says no, but rather yes, not yet, or I've got something better. Believing that HP loves me unconditionally has changed my life.

— *Pennsylvania USA*

# My Daily Prayer

I would like to share with my fellow OA members a prayer I wrote to help me strengthen my daily contact with my HP. Each morning, I set aside 15 minutes while having breakfast to read my *For Today* book, followed by this prayer. I find this helps put my thinking in perspective and my trust in HP for the rest of the day.

Dear God,

Just for today, let me be willing to hand my life and will over to you totally, feeling secure and protected in the knowledge that your love for me is unconditional, trusting that your plan for me today is to lead me one small step nearer recovery. No matter what today brings, I know you are watching over me, and you will guide and protect me.

Let me feel the joy of knowing that for the next twenty-four hours—if I'm willing to admit my powerlessness and hand my life and will over to you—in return I will receive freedom and relief from the pain and bondage that trying to control life, people, and my weight has caused me. Just for today, if I can believe that all I need to do is work the OA Steps to the best of my ability and live as simply as possible, I will receive the wonderful gifts of abstinence, serenity, and sanity and be filled with the warmth and security of your unconditional love.

Thank you, God, for giving me this very special day.

— *Dubai, United Arab Emirates*

# The Gratitude Path

It seems to me that the antidote to negative thinking is gratitude. I tend toward negativity, especially when I'm confused or stressed. I find that if I substitute thoughts of gratitude, my thinking goes from being fear-based to being God-based. By thinking myself into a state of gratitude, I am freed of my negativity.

It doesn't matter how childish or mundane my thanks are. I can begin with thoughts such as these: Thank you for the chair. Thank you for the stars. Thank you for my shoes. Thank you for the opportunity to serve. Thank you for new challenges. Thank you for guidance. These thoughts help me get out of my negative feelings and concentrate on that for which I am grateful. Then I end up in a spiritually high place, where I'm in a state of gratitude. Rather than taking all my blessings for granted, I feel the presence of a power greater than myself. I don't feel alone, vulnerable, insignificant, or negative. Instead, I feel full of faith, safe, and confident that I'm on the right path.

— *Louisiana USA*

# Thankful Prayers

I've been working to rediscover my Higher Power. Food had become my God, and I worshipped it regularly. With the miracle of OA, I have come to believe again that faith in a Higher Power can restore me to sanity. The call of food is still loud and demanding some days, but the desire to binge and overeat is becoming less. Praying to my Higher Power has become my personal tool, which I use many times each day.

*Praying to my Higher Power has become my personal tool.*

At first, my prayers were asking something of God. Please give me motivation, a quick weight loss, and the power to control my eating. This approach was not working, because I wanted God to do all the work. Why wasn't God answering my requests? Then I found an article in the *Lifeline Sampler* ("The Second Miracle," p.105) that said to be thankful when you pray.

To start, I kept it simple: "Thank You, God, for giving me another day to do your will. Thank you for helping me eat sensibly throughout the day." Then I ran into a roadblock of anger and resentments.

I have much anger toward my mother, who lives with me. This anger goes back a long way. Nothing I did seemed to please her. Even though I made better grades in school than my siblings, she said she expected more from me because my first-grade teacher said I had the potential to be an A student. When I graduated third in my high-school class, she said I purposely didn't graduate first because I didn't want to give a speech. Nothing I did was ever good enough.

Now my mother lives with me. I pay the bills and she takes care of the house. If I do something around the house to help, she complains that I'm not doing it right. But if I don't do anything, she says I don't help enough. She sends mixed messages, so I leave the house to her.

A couple of weeks ago, Mom got upset with me, and I was angry in return. I stayed angry for days. Then I remembered the article in the *Sampler* and decided to try again. The first day I was thankful that I had a mother. I did not want to be without her no matter how critical she was. The next day I found more things about my mother to be thankful for. She is always there when I need her. She runs errands and keeps the house clean. Each day I found more things about my mother that I was truly thankful for. As I continued my thanking process, I realized that I was thankful for many things in my life.

It has been a revelation. When I start thinking positively about life, I realize how much worse it could be. By using my OA tools,

I've learned to prioritize things in my day, and to work on those things first. I've tried to do at least one thing each week around the house to organize my personal belongings. Last weekend I cleaned the desk and organized everything. I found something I had bought four years ago and hadn't been able to find. I've started exercising again. Last weekend, my mother complimented me. She said OA was really helping me, I had made much progress, and she hoped I would continue with the program.

This was a miracle for me. I believe this is a result of my thankful prayers. Thank God for my mother, whom I love dearly, and thank God for OA, which has helped me realize that I have many positive things in my life.

— *Illinois USA*

# CHAPTER SIX

# By the Grace of God

*Higher Power's love and acceptance brought profound
changes to the lives of these OA members.*

# Humility, Forgiveness, and Step Seven

The basic ingredient of humility is a desire to seek and do God's will. My humble admission of my powerlessness over compulsive overeating was my first step toward liberation from its paralyzing grip.

The Step-Seven Prayer (*Alcoholics Anonymous*, 4th ed., p. 76) says, "My Creator, I am now willing that you should have all of me, good and bad. I pray that you now remove from me every single defect of character which stands in the way of my usefulness to you and my fellows. Grant me strength, as I go out from here, to do your bidding. Amen."

Through Step Seven, I know God has forgiven me for my past, and I have forgiven myself. To forgive means to pass over an offense and free the offender from the judgment deserved. Clearly, I need to go on forgiving and forgiving, as God forgives me for my past mistakes.

> *To forgive is hard; to live with the consequences of not forgiving is harder.*

All I need to do is tell him of my wrongs. The more I trust that God forgives and continues to show me love and mercy, the easier it is for me to forgive others. To forgive is hard; to live with the consequences of not forgiving is harder.

In choosing to forgive, I commit myself never to bring up the offense again, but instead to act kindly toward the offender, as described in "Freedom From Bondage" in the Big Book (*Alcoholics Anonymous*, 4th ed., pp. 544-552). I do this, not because the offender deserves it, but because doing so fulfills God's will and brings me personal freedom.

As I acknowledge my wrongs to God, he takes away my guilt but does not remove the consequences of the event. I remain responsible for my actions as well as my reactions.

Through Step Seven, I am challenged further to put away all bitter thoughts, along with the desire to get even. I've found that bitterness is a way I punish myself for someone else's offense against me. Bitterness is unresolved anger and the refusal to forgive, and it eats away at me.

When I realized that I have wronged God far more than others have wronged me—and I've been forgiven—I am freed from the bondage of arrogance so I can forgive others. It always helps to remember that, in the eyes of God, I am a forgiven person.

— *Pennsylvania USA*

# A Spiritual Choice

In my lifetime, I have had a tendency to manufacture a lot of my own misery. I don't think I did it on purpose, but my stubborn will and pride often got in the way. By clinging to my way of doing things, I created a lot of headaches and heartaches that probably could have been avoided.

I am grateful to OA that for today, and, I hope, for the rest of my life, I am abstinent. Actually, I'd rather say I'm choosing to be abstinent. In some ways abstinence is a gift, and in others, a choice. For me, the gift is freedom from obsession with body image and with food—where to get it, eat it, hide it, purge it. That gift was given to me by God, and I believe it says somewhere in our literature that we maintain that gift through our spiritual condition. I know I'm not always free of these obsessions, especially when things seem overwhelming in my life. That's when abstinence, for me, becomes a choice.

This disease manifests itself in various forms in different people—starving, bingeing, overexercising, vomiting—but a lot of it is about control. When I want to control my life because I can't wait for God's direction, and when things aren't going my way, I turn to other sources instead of resting in his care.

But looking back over the past five years in OA, I can see that he's always worked things out for my good. I do not believe my Higher Power always wants me to be happy. I believe he wants what's best for me, and sometimes that just doesn't make me happy—like when I have to wait for something I want, when I have to take a pay cut to get a more fulfilling and less stressful job, or when he wants me to marry a frog (who has turned into quite a prince). My Higher Power wants only the best for me, and when I take over, I miss his best.

When I was twenty-five and forty thousand dollars in debt, he got me into a free treatment program, provided places for me to live, a car to drive, food to eat, a job, and then OA. He took care of me long before I believed he would.

When I met my fiancé, I thought it would never work. He was a blue-collar man, he hunted, and he drove a truck! I wanted a yuppie who drove a BMW and wore a tie to work. But my handsome prince is the most sincere, humble, gentle, kind, and thoughtful man I've ever met; in three months I'll be his wife.

The most recent miracle is my job. I'd been in a job that I hated for three years. But I couldn't give up the money, the travel, and the prestige it afforded … until I couldn't take the emotional stress anymore. It took me three years to let go of my will, but within days of my surrender, the job I've always wanted at this company has been handed to me on a silver platter. (Not gold, mind you, because I'm taking a cut in pay, and I think I have to give up my car phone!) I haven't been this excited about work in years.

I owe it all to my Higher Power and to OA. I truly believe in the Third and Eleventh Steps: that if I pray for willingness, sometimes even the willingness to pray for willingness, my Higher Power is faithful. And thank you to everyone in OA for being there to help me as I grow. I couldn't stay abstinent without you—without meetings, sponsors, phone calls, and all the rest. You've been there to hold my hand as I've cried and thought I would lose my mind. You've encouraged me to keep coming back. You've listened and loved me through it all. I'm so grateful to you. I just wanted you to know.

— *Wisconsin USA*

## Connections

I have enjoyed the articles I've read in *Lifeline* on spirituality, but I've felt that something was missing. I read lots of great things about God and spirituality and meditation, but it all felt pretty generic. What I missed was how this generic spirituality connects to recovery from overeating.

*My spiritual development began when I put the fork down.*

It is easy to get confused about the spiritual nature of the OA program. As it says in *Our Invitation to You,* we have a threefold illness: physical, emotional, spiritual. It then goes on to say that our program is spiritual. Period. It does not say that our recovery program is threefold, only spiritual. However, this doesn't mean that if we sit on a mountaintop and contemplate our navels, we will never have to think about the physical and emotional aspects of our lives. The emotional, physical, and spiritual dimensions of our being are interconnected; what we do in one area affects us in other areas as well.

Every spiritual path includes physical and emotional disciplines as tools for spiritual development. Not one of them says that gluttony is the path to spiritual enlightenment. My spiritual development began when I put the fork down. I was 110 pounds (50 kg) overweight, and bingeing on massive quantities of candy. My brain was so fogged by the sugar that I was emotionally and spiritually numb. Prayer was something only "weirdos" did.

Out of desperation, I came to OA, willing to do anything to escape the living hell of morbid obesity. I got abstinent by getting a sponsor who suggested I go to ninety meetings in ninety days; stop eating my binge foods and all forms of sugar; phone in my food every day; and start reading AA's Big Book. It worked. As I started abstaining, the fog started to lift. I let go of my preconceived ideas and started doing what I saw working for others. I noticed that the people who had what I wanted had worked all Twelve Steps of the program, including a written Fourth Step; used lots of prayer and meditation; and worked with others. I noticed they did not eat the foods that caused them problems. My weight came off, and I've been maintaining that weight loss in OA for over twelve years.

One of the benefits of spirituality is feeling at peace with the universe—knowing who I am and knowing all is right with me and God. Eating just the right amount of food, not too much and not too little, is part of staying right-sized both spiritually and physically. Weighing and measuring my food is a spiritual act of acceptance that I am an overeater; it's not the futile attempt at control it was in my dieting days.

The spirituality of OA is not something we do alone, by ourselves, in our own kitchens. We must carry the message to other overeaters, or we will die. The Big Book says, "faith without works is dead." By reaching out to other overeaters, I get outside my own self-centered universe, furthering my spiritual growth. That is why half the tools of recovery are about ways of connecting with other overeaters: phone calls, service, sponsorship, meetings. Working closely with others shows us clearly what works and what doesn't. It leads to a healthy dose of joyful living.

It's easy to get caught up in arguments about which part of our recovery is most important—the physical, emotional, or spiritual. The answer is whichever part is missing. The three are so interconnected, that if one part is missing, the other two parts are severely stunted. Recovery from overeating can be compared to a three-legged stool: one leg is physical, another leg is spiritual, the third is emotional. If any leg is missing, the stool topples over.

— *Virginia USA*


# What a Relief!

I've been a compulsive overeater all my life. My forty years before OA were filled with self-loathing; I didn't believe I had anything of worth to give anyone else. I found myself wishing I wouldn't live past thirty years of age.

Now, I thank God that I did. I am maintaining a 70-pound (32-kg) weight loss after two years in the program. Through OA and my Higher Power, I've found a sense of peace that I never knew before. I am happy to be alive. I wake up each morning and thank God for another day, and I mean it. I accept challenges as growth-producing and welcome them with a grateful heart. I love myself now, and I can admit to my character defects without coming down on myself like a ton of bricks for being imperfect.

And what a relief it is not to have to be perfect! I found that doing the Fourth and Fifth Steps and making amends were liberating. I felt a heavy load lifted from me, and I walk straighter now and have a smile on my face that is genuine.

I have my own version of the Serenity Prayer that has given me many peaceful and sleep-filled nights. (This is new for me, too.) "God, grant me the serenity to accept myself as I am and as I was, the courage to change in the way you wish me to, and the wisdom to allow you to do it. Amen."

I never dreamed all this would happen. I never thought I could be at peace and believe in a God who loves me. OA has done this for me.

— *Anonymous*

# Asking for Transformation

"Please, God, restore me to sanity." Whether I say these words in belief or disbelief seems not to matter. God doesn't care whether I believe or not, as long as I speak truthfully and from my heart when I speak to him. God is so powerful that he effects change through his spirit, which enters me and changes my thought patterns instantaneously, without my even being aware of it. I need only ask, and I become changed.

My insanity extends beyond food obsession and destructive eating. It includes fearful thoughts, paranoia about what others think and might do to me, and a general blindness to the destructive patterns in my life.

After a prayer, my sanity is restored, sometimes in a flash, sometimes more slowly. When I'm waking from sleep, for example, I will have a revelation about just how insane I've been about food and my life. At other times, I'll have small moments of increasing comfort with people, or I'll be able to disregard insane fantasies about whether a person I care about is annoyed with me. This healing comes as a gift from God himself—not through some psychological process, but through grace.

*I have many unanswered, maybe unanswerable, questions about God.*

I must keep my feet on the ground, however. I am human and must get my head out of the clouds and do what I call "taking care of business"—going to work, facing fearful situations, talking to other OA members when I feel out of sorts, exercising regularly, and making phone calls in desperate moments. These are all critical to my success as a healing person.

I have many unanswered, maybe unanswerable, questions about God. Where is he when I talk to him? Does he speak through other people? Does God predetermine life span and time of death? These are things I need not worry about now. I just try to be humble enough to ask for help and to carry out my hunches when God's spirit has moved me.

Thanks to OA, I have six years of freedom from bulimia. My recovery has led me to this awareness about a Higher Power. I am very grateful for the peace.

— *Anonymous*

## Serenity to the Nth Degree

I've been in program for a number of years, but the number isn't important to me. Today, this very moment is most important.

I used to feel that I was either better than or less than other people, but those days are fading; I'm discovering that knowing God is a good-enough achievement. The roadmap he has designed for my life does not make my story unique, but it has made me grateful for all that happens and gives me the power to treat all people with love and dignity.

When I first came to program, I did as I had always done—took everyone's inventory. But soon life showed me that it was possible to handle pain without food. I slowly realized that all my character defects worked for me in one way or another. They are not mistakes. I'm not a mistake. I truly believe that there are no mistakes. I'm not better than or less than anyone else. I just am, and to me, that's serenity to the nth degree.

I have learned, through this program, how to forgive through acceptance. I have, at times, detached with love when an expectation arises. I'm grateful to be in OA, one day at a time.

— *North Carolina USA*

# Fed from Within

When I first came to OA, my program was a food plan and meetings. I also exercised. These were enough to take off pounds, but not to keep them off.

*My food is spiritual.*

For the next decade, I went deeper, learning to recognize feelings and how to cope with them. When I was angry, I saw that I "ate at" people instead of confronting them. When I was fearful, I ran away into food. No matter what the feeling—lonely, depressed, hurt, self-hating, guilty, deprived, worried—I used food to bury it. Since I was "abstinent" and didn't overeat, I maintained my weight loss.

Gradually, I learned healthy alternatives. When I was envious, I realized that the person I envied was someone to learn from. Loneliness didn't mean I needed other people; it was a sign that I was alienated from myself. Boredom signaled that I was understimulated. When I found a challenging book, I felt mentally fed and my hunger vanished. Slowly, I substituted emotional and mental sustenance for food.

In this decade, my food is spiritual. Because I've surrendered my will, because my heart has been opened by twenty-six years of sharing with thousands of OA members, I am now fed by:

- Gratitude: I am grateful for simple things, for being grateful, for being alive, for being me. I don't need success to feel grateful.

- Coincidence: Constant serendipity reinforces the feeling that I am moving in the right direction.

- Connection: I sense a close bond among the different aspects of myself and between my Higher Power and me.

- Meaning: The world is no longer a jumble. I find pattern and divine order in everything.

- Trust: I know that despite the dangers around me, I am protected by being connected.

- Faith: I feel that God has ordained me to do the work I do and that my Higher Power is helping me attain my life's purpose.

- Guidance: At the right time, God is leading me to the people, places and things I need or is attracting them to me. This has happened so many times that now I cannot deny it.

- Serenity: I have serenity attacks often. I feel calm and assured for no apparent reason.

- Peace of mind: The internalized self-hate is gone. I am my own best friend. I encourage myself.

- Contentment: Although the world seems to be getting more brutal and mechanical, I am convinced that God is still in charge. I do what I can to brighten my corner, but I no longer feel hungry because everything appears to be going downhill.

- Love: I am God's child, and I am loved and cared for daily. God knows what I need better than I do, and he wants me to have it even more than I do.

- Inspiration: I am given what I need when I need it. I am in the flow of divine ideas. Because I have emptied myself of self, I can be receptive to spiritual food. I am now a vessel; I am fed from within.

— *California USA*

# Formula Folly

I don't know if it's true, but I heard recently that farmers have a formula for planting, but not for harvesting. They till the soil, fertilize, plant the seed, spray the pesticides, remove the weeds, and sometimes water the ground as well. Then they wait. Eventually they find themselves at harvest time, and they gather it in. The farmer is expected to work the soil the best he can. He is not expected to produce the harvest. The harvest occurs because of natural laws: not understood, but greatly appreciated.

As I reflect on my history in OA, I can see that what may be true of the farmer is certainly true for me. Whenever I've made the harvest my focus, I've fallen. When I took responsibility for the harvest, it vanished. I now understand that this is because God is the boss of my harvest. It is by God's grace, not my efforts, that I have any semblance of recovery: physical, emotional, or spiritual. My recovery did not come about by my wonderful adherence to the Steps or diligent use of the tools. The Steps and tools are merely preparing the "soil" of my heart. The recovery harvest occurred by the grace of God. I don't understand how the planting and harvesting principle works, but I am deeply grateful that it does.

— *Anonymous*

# The Teacher Appears

"When we look back, we realize that the things which came to us when we put ourselves in God's hands were better than anything we could have planned" (*Alcoholics Anonymous*, 4th ed., p. 100).

One night my Higher Power presented me with Life Lesson #3,498. What a beautiful lesson it was, presented lovingly.

I've been blessed with membership in OA for more than ten

years. The gifts I've received in OA are greater than words could ever say. The most obvious is the maintenance of a 250-pound (114-kg) weight loss. That gift, however, is minor compared to the others.

One of the great joys in my life has been my career as an elementary school teacher. I've taught for twenty-six years, and program has enabled me to greet each day as an opportunity to learn and to love. "When the student is ready, the teacher appears."

God sent a ten-year-old teacher to bring me the lesson. This little girl, a former student of mine, came to visit one night. She had saved her allowance to buy me a special present: a miniature Winnie the Pooh figurine. It warmed my heart and soul.

*God sent a ten-year-old teacher to bring me the lesson.*

How does my lesson fit in here? This child has known me only in recovery. She has seen only the person who strives to be patient, tolerant, loving, and kind. She never knew the selfish, raging woman I was when food was my god. The love she showed me had a tremendous impact, more than the gift itself. Later, while sharing at my OA meeting, I realized that as much as this child loves the "me" she knows, God must love me much more. God loves not only the "me" in recovery; he also loved the horrible, vengeful person I was in disease. That night I learned what the grace of God means.

My mind could not comprehend the wondrous changes that would take place in my life thanks to the love and grace of my Higher Power. I did not earn these things. God gave them to me simply because I am. To have these miracles, all I have to do is work my program.

— *Florida USA*

# True Blessings

*As I soar to the heights in the air,*
*And dive to the depths of despair,*
*I find there is a power with me*
*Until the very end.*

*One who never leaves me,*
*No matter where I go,*
*The one who takes care of*
*The part that is my soul.*

*No matter how deep I dive,*
*Nor how high I soar,*
*There is one who's waiting*
*To lead me down the road.*

*The one who watches over*
*My time here on earth*
*Will heal my wounds, my hurts,*
*And ease my every fear.*

*Nowhere can I go alone,*
*Nor can I hurt and cry alone,*
*For he is always with me*
*To lead me down the road.*

*When I feel I am put to the test,*
*And can go no further in my humanness,*
*There he is to hold me,*
*And in his arms I rest.*

*Thank you, dear spirit, for guiding*
*My soul to you for rest,*
*And for taking my brokenness*
*Within you to bless.*

*And thank you for leading me*
*Into the fellowship of my friends*
*Who help me learn to listen and to heal,*
*Who teach me how to follow the Steps to recovery.*

*No longer alone, no longer lost,*
*I have truly been blessed*
*With a power to love and guide me,*
*Twelve Steps to lead me,*
*And friends who will remind me,*
*This too shall pass.*

*— Oklahoma USA*

# New Spiritual Strength

I joined OA in 1991 in Houston, Texas, because I was tired of diet groups, nutritionists, and all the other ways I knew of losing weight. I wanted to be healthy for my retirement life, which my husband and I would soon begin.

We moved back home to California, where I found many OA groups. I then began my new spiritual journey. Even though my home meeting was on my Sabbath, I felt it was my way of having a special time to communicate with God.

> *When I attend services, the beauty and meaning of my faith affect me more than ever before.*

Through OA, I learned that I have a personal God, one I can speak to in my own words and to whom I feel a strong connection. My new spiritual strength has given me a stronger religious sense. As I look at prayers I've spoken for years, I see the same language that I find in OA. When I attend services, the beauty and meaning of my faith affect me more than ever before.

My husband, who is a normal eater, has also become more spiritual through my spirituality in OA. We start the day holding each other and saying prayers to God for giving us life this day. At dinner we hold hands and silently pray together.

More important, our love for each other has grown deeper through our loving care and respect. My husband supports my recovery and enjoys all the changes he has seen in me since I came to OA. He especially likes what I learned at a retreat: "If you want a loving husband, be a loving wife," and vice versa.

— *Anonymous*

# How I Found Joy

"The joy of living is the theme of AA's Twelfth Step, and action is its key word." This sentence begins the chapter on Step Twelve in AA's "Twelve and Twelve." The chapter describes the wondrous new way of life that is ours as a result of working the Steps and having had a spiritual awakening. It reminds me that the ultimate goal of working the OA program includes finding a profound joy that overflows and touches those around us.

I once scoffed at the idea that life could be joyful, even while I was abstinent and working the Steps. I felt robbed when members with long-term abstinence talked about having peace and happiness or when a speaker read the promises.

My disbelief had two sources: misunderstanding what joy means, and several years of being abstinent, yet emotionally miserable. I have always confused joy with happiness. I thought the goal of life was to be happy every day. I don't think that way anymore. To me, joy is a river, a perpetually flowing undercurrent in my life. It is peace, serenity, trust, and faith. It flows so deeply inside me that I sometimes forget it is there. Happiness is a spring that occasionally bursts forth from my river. It is fleeting, temporary, and spontaneous—wonderful when I can have it, but not necessary. Joy keeps me grounded and peaceful.

Several years ago I heard in a meeting that "if you're working the program and you're still not happy, you're doing something wrong." I decided that what I was doing wrong was not taking enough action. I was working the Steps, but not applying them to my daily life except around food.

Once I took action to relieve my loneliness, it quickly abated. I started saying the first three Steps around relationships. "I am powerless over my fear of people, and I cannot manage relationships; but I believe, Lord God, that you can restore me to sanity. Therefore, I turn over my will and my life to your care. Whatever you tell me to do to get out of this place, I will do, with your help." To my great surprise, he rapidly gave me answers. I followed his direction and am seldom lonely today. I have new friendships that are deeply fulfilling, my old ones are improving, and I am learning to reach out even when it scares me. Just as the AA "Twelve and Twelve" says, action was the key to finding joy in living.

Now that I have redefined joy for myself and have begun to take more action, the joy of living is real for me. I am still miserable in some areas of my life, and that reminds me that I need to take action. Mostly I feel peaceful. Sometimes my joy is a river, and sometimes it's a fountain. Most days have plenty of happiness "springs." As long as I continue to be honest, take action, and stay open to change, I find the river of joy never stops deepening, widening, and lengthening. It is endless because it comes from HP, and HP's love is endless.

— *Virginia USA*

# CHAPTER SEVEN

〰〰〰〰〰〰〰〰〰〰〰〰〰〰〰〰

■

# Agnostics and Atheists: A Unique Perspective

*Some OA members found the spiritual principles of the program challenging—and surprisingly uplifting.*

# A Nonbeliever

I no longer believe in a personal god. I did not always believe this way; when I came to OA almost ten years ago, I strongly believed in a Higher Power to whom I could turn over my life. Many incidents occurred in this past year, however, that have banished this belief entirely.

But the strange thing is that I still have a deep, if not more profound, spiritual life than I had before. I just don't depend on a god to do my work for me. I read the OA pamphlet, *What If I Don't Believe in God?* and it has been helpful. I also found the Big Book's chapter "To the Agnostic" useful as well.

I've done some writing on the Steps, trying to adjust them to my new belief system, and it has proved very difficult, especially Steps Two and Three. The sanity I hope to have restored is about getting to know myself better; it is about clearing out those nasty defects of character so I can be open to the movement of spirit within me, to develop my personality to its greatest level. To maintain abstinence is paramount to me, otherwise my mind will not be clear enough to understand life's teachings. Step Seven has also proved difficult—to whom do I turn over my defects? I figured I could release them to the universe and develop myself to a deeper level through meditation.

These are just a few of the ways I've handled problems regarding this new belief of mine. My abstinence has been good throughout this period. I've also looked to the spirit of the Fellowship as part of my new spirituality. Many times I will turn things over to this spirit.

I am interested in hearing how others who do not believe in a personal god devote themselves to the OA way of life. I would like to know how other nonbelievers handle the Twelve Steps and "turning it over." I hope that others will write to *Lifeline*, using it as one forum for those of us with an alternative way of living the Steps.

— *Pennsylvania USA*

# Even for the Faithless

The basic difference between people who believe in God and those who don't is that believers are able to accept the existence of God as an article of faith—a belief that does not rest on seemingly logical proof or evidence. I will not make such a leap of faith in God, as we conventionally understand the meaning of the word "God," without more clear and convincing evidence.

*How can I, a confirmed atheist, work this program?*

How then can I, a confirmed atheist, work this program, which so often invokes the name of God, instructs us to pray to God, and directs us to turn our will and our lives over to the care of God?

For five years now, I've been going to meetings, following a plan of eating, making daily phone calls, giving service, reading literature, meditating, and enjoying the benefits of abstinence from compulsive eating. I started at 400 pounds (182 kg), and for well over three years have weighed around 175 pounds (80 kg). Not only am I in very good physical shape, but most of the time I am emotionally and, yes, spiritually at peace. How can this be if I don't have a Higher Power?

People like me are fortunate that ours is not a religious program; rather, it is a spiritual program. It makes room, if only barely, for those of us who are not theists; those like me who do not believe in a personal God, creator, or ruler of the world. Admittedly, some passages in our literature (the Third- and Seventh-Step prayers, for example) cause me mild distress, and I feel excluded when my fellow sufferers choose to close the circle of our Fellowship with a prayer that represents their Higher Power. But I remain secure in the knowledge that this program works for me, in spite of my lack of acceptance for religion.

Perhaps it works for me because I am not, in fact, without a Higher Power. I know that I could not do what I've done, day by day, alone. I place my faith, trust, and dependence in a power greater than myself that was initially based on the experience of others who came before me, and is now rooted in my own experience of the past five years. I now have an abstinence from compulsive eating that far exceeds anything I previously was able to do on my own.

Today, my hope and security is in the Fellowship of Overeaters Anonymous. The collective "you" are not my "God," but Overeaters Anonymous is my Higher Power. I have found that when two or more powerless compulsive eaters sit together in a room, read the Twelve Steps and Twelve Traditions, and share their experience honestly, the sum of our powers far exceeds our ineffective individual power. It's kind of like magic; it's not entirely reasonable. But the fact remains that we can do together what none of us has been able to do alone.

— *Washington USA*


# Light at the Top of the Pit

Not so long ago, I lived my life as though I were lying at the bottom of a deep, dark pit. When I looked up, I could see sunlight at the top of this pit, but it was far, far away. Most of the time I did not have the energy or the motivation to even lift myself off the floor. I did not have any strength. It seemed like I only had barely enough strength to breathe. Occasionally, I would try to get up and crawl up the side of the pit. I would only get a few inches off the bottom when the dirt would break loose, and I would fall again. Then, finally, I gave up trying. But I always looked up and saw sunlight at the top of the pit. I didn't know back then what that sunlight represented. I did not find that out until I walked through the doors of OA.

In OA I discovered, with the help of the loving, caring Fellowship and the Twelve-Step program, that the sunlight was God. In my whole life, I never believed in a God; I never believed in any higher power at all until I was forty years old and discovered OA. Once I found God, he gave me an immeasurable amount of freedom, strength, and energy. He gave me the strength to climb out, one hand above the other and one step after the other. One day at a time, I crawled out of that pit.

The closer I came to the top, the more beautiful the sunlight was: the sunlight that represented God's love for me. I would have never found God if it had not been for the wonderful people I met in OA. The unconditional love I received, the caring, and the sharing of experiences turned my life around—literally, completely around.

> *The unconditional love I received, the caring, and the sharing of experiences turned my life around.*

I've been in OA for one year, and I've just completed going through my Twelve Steps. I have a wonderful, caring, loving sponsor I can turn to and a wonderful Fellowship that I've found in OA. I now have a patient, loving, and strong God in my life. Once I gave up my self-will to God and tried to live my life according to his plan for me, I began to lose the weight. I began to pray that my character defects be removed. My obsession with food was removed.

One day at a time, my whole life has changed. I've lost 87 pounds (40 kg), and I now exercise every day. I love the support and the sharing at OA meetings. I try to attend four meetings a week, and I want to express how grateful I am to all of the Fellowship at all of the meetings. I'm grateful to OA for showing me that there is a Higher Power, a loving and caring God who can and will change your life.

Don't ever give up. God is out there; all you have to do is ask for help and he will give it to you. I am living proof of that. I do have occasional slips and relapses, but I know deeply in my heart that I will never go back to the way I was before I found God, before I found OA. I never want to lose the spirituality I now have. I know that a slip or a relapse can happen, and I tell myself, "This too shall pass," and it does.

I wrote this story for other atheists who are struggling with compulsive overeating and don't know where to turn or what to do. In addition, I wrote to convey this message to younger women: don't wait! You don't have to wait until you're forty years old to walk through the doors of an OA meeting. The sooner you attend the meetings, the sooner you can start, with God's help and guidance, to turn your life around. Believe me, there is light at the top of that pit, and that light is God. May you find him now.

— *Pennsylvania USA*

## Spiritual Progression

I am someone who "came for the vanity and stayed for the sanity." I came to my first OA meeting in 1986 after thirteen years of bingeing and dieting, and I've stayed ever since. The people at my first meeting had something I wanted. I didn't know what it was then, but now I know it was peace of mind. I was nervous because OA was a spiritual program and I was an atheist. They assured me I could pick a Higher Power of my understanding. Mostly, I was scared and sick of hiding my bingeing, of being obsessed with my weight, of not being able to stick to a diet more than a few days.

*I was nervous because OA was a spiritual program and I was an atheist.*

I was a lukewarm member for two years. I attended meetings irregularly and chose a sponsor, but I didn't work with her. I would abstain from compulsive overeating at times, but the times always ended. Finally, I realized I would have to put down the fork. I committed to working with a sponsor, to trying to abstain from my binge foods, and to eating three moderate meals a day. I started attending more meetings, gave service, and committed to writing my Fourth Step and giving it away.

It worked! I released the excess weight and have maintained a 35-to-40 pound (16-to-18 kg) weight loss for more than eleven years. My program hasn't been perfect, but I have kept coming back, especially in hard times (mostly because I was scared to go out there; leaving didn't seem to work for others). I keep coming back because it is a joy, because I have a short memory and might forget I'm a compulsive eater, and because I have a responsibility to share what worked for me with others who still suffer.

The greatest benefit of my recovery has been my progression from atheist to a person with a faith system. My faith is my anchor, and my outlook on life has changed since I came in. I don't belong to a structured spiritual organization, but coming to know a God of my understanding has been the major joy of my recovery.

— *Anonymous*

# CHAPTER EIGHT

# Tools for Spiritual Growth

*These OA members use the Steps, the tools,
and literature to grow spiritually.*

# The Steps to Freedom

I was intrigued by your suggestion in the October 1995 issue of *Lifeline* for readers to write articles about some aspect of the program they would like to see the magazine address. When I thought about this, I realized that I would like to see how other OA members work the Steps in their daily lives. How do the Steps all work together to free us each day from our obsession with food? How do they help us lead the lives our Higher Power intended for us?

The Big Book has helped me do this in my life. At the meetings I attend, we've focused lately on the uncomplicated set of instructions in those first 164 pages. I have been in OA almost twelve years now, and thought I knew what it meant to work the Steps, but I realized that most of my time was spent on the tools, not the Steps. I am beginning to see that the tools are there to help me work the Steps. They don't have any magic of their own.

*When I ask God's forgiveness at night, I sleep well and wake up rested, without baggage from the previous day.*

Lately, I've found the suggestions on page 86 of the Big Book most useful. "When we retire at night, we constructively review the day" (*Alcoholics Anonymous*, 4th ed.) Each night, I ask myself those questions about being resentful, dishonest, and afraid. As a result, I've discovered that I can stay more honest with my feelings, my food plan, and my relationships. This practice helps me focus on what I have given to the world today. I need this reminder because it's so easy for me to fall into a negative self-centeredness. As I asked myself these questions last night, I realized that even though I am at home recuperating from surgery, I can still be of service. I decided to write this article, which is a lot more fun than sitting around feeling sorry for myself. When I examine my actions and ask God's forgiveness at night, I sleep well and wake up rested, without baggage from the previous day.

"On awakening let us think about the twenty-four hours ahead." This suggestion, also from page 86 in the Big Book, helps me think about my day—what I will face at work, any potentially dangerous food situations, any amends I need to make—and then I ask God to direct my thinking. I follow this with some reading from a daily meditation book and write God a letter about what I am feeling.

This is how I acknowledge my need for God's help in managing all areas of my life. I invite him to heal all parts of me that need mending. It keeps me humble, yet light of heart and spirit. I'd like to say that I do this every day without fail, but I don't. I get rebellious, my life gets too full, and I would sometimes rather read the paper. But then I start to feel out of sorts, so I pick up this "kit of spiritual tools" once again—with gratitude.

— *New York USA*


# God Always Shows Up

I've listened to inventories in the small, private chapel at the hospital where my home group meets. I've heard inventories in public parks, my backyard, a sponsoree's kitchen while the baby slept, even in restaurants. I've shared my own inventories with a sponsor at her workplace, over the telephone with new and old friends, and in a Twelfth-Step-Within group. I've given them away and heard them in installments as well as in day-long sessions.

But no matter what the variables, one thing is always the same. I'm aware of the presence of a Power greater than myself in these situations, whether I'm on the giving or receiving end of Step Five. Step Five says that we admit "to God, to ourselves and to another human being the exact nature of our wrongs." If I show up and another human being shows up, it is my experience that God always shows up for this spiritual cleansing.

As I listened to a Fifth Step one time in the little hospital chapel, a sponsoree told me about an extremely painful difficulty in her life. We were both in tears—she because she saw no way out, and I because I empathized with her suffering. When my sponsoree had completed her Fifth Step, we both decided we would go to the meeting, which had already started, even though we were late and teary-eyed.

*We both became aware of a steadily increasing sense of peace, connection, and well-being.*

But her pain was raw and potent. We had to do something for closure before going in to the meeting. We decided to take the risk that we wouldn't be interrupted and held hands to pray together. I began and then she continued, her voice barely audible through the sobs. Then we sat quietly for a moment. Slowly, we both became aware of a steadily increasing sense of peace, connection, and well-being. Within a few minutes, we went in to the meeting together.

Over the next few weeks, this woman told me how Step Seven was working on her seemingly unsolvable problem. Step Seven really is a miracle. But I've seen that this miracle can't occur unless we complete the usually terrifying and humbling Fifth Step. It has catapulted my own recovery more than I can say to be able to help other people through this process.

A thorough Fourth and Fifth Step preceded my being "rocketed into the fourth dimension." In other words, they were what gave me freedom from the compulsion to overeat. I shared a particularly nasty inventory with a friend about the attitudes I had inherited from both my parents about food, eating, and body size. It took me a few hours to write and about fifteen minutes to read. The next day, I ate a moderate breakfast followed by a moderate lunch (at a potluck, no less!) followed by a moderate dinner. This pattern of moderation continued for days, then for weeks, then for months as I worked the rest of the Steps. Soon I will celebrate nine years of continuous abstinence.

If you haven't experienced this wonderful opportunity for spiritual growth, I recommend two things. One, do your own Fourth and Fifth Steps. Then, two, tell others in the program of the benefits of sharing an inventory, and tell them you are available to listen to theirs. You won't be sorry.

— *Anonymous*


# Not Work, Just Life

I am very grateful to have Overeaters Anonymous in my life. In fact, I can safely say that OA gives me a life. Today I do things, go places, and take risks. Without the help of OA's plan for living, I would have stayed locked in fear. My obsession with food and my body is but a symptom of my spiritual malady. I need OA's Twelve Steps, Twelve Traditions, and tools to participate fully in life. I need to work my program to arrest my illness and grow closer to my Higher Power's will for me.

> *God speaks to me, but he does not work for me.*

First and foremost, I need a plan of eating. I have learned that unless I put down the foods that cause binges and trigger my body and weight obsession, I cannot hear my Higher Power. Food cuts me off from God. It also keeps me from myself, my friends, and my family. Because God speaks to me through others in and outside of the OA rooms, I must put down the food if I am to listen.

God speaks to me, but he does not work for me. This means that I'm responsible for my food choices. I make a grocery list and go to the store to ensure I will have abstinent foods in my house. I pack my lunch in the evening when I make supper. When I travel, I call the airline and request a vegetarian or diabetic meal because they are usually healthier than the regular meals. I pack extra water and abstinent foods.

To keep emotionally fit, I rely on the tools and the Steps. I use writing to find out what's going on with me. How am I feeling? Why am I resentful? What are my expectations, and are they different from my Higher Power's? I go to meetings and share my feelings with people who love me unconditionally. I call my sponsor to talk about my fears and anxieties.

The Steps help me keep my emotions from taking over. Steps Four and Ten work best to keep me honest and aware. If I'm anxious about a project, practicing Step Three and letting the anxiety go will help. If I'm angry at a person or a group of people, I can take a Fourth Step and find out what my part is. Before OA, I ate over every feeling; now I have many other options to deal with my emotions.

My relationship with my Higher Power, the spiritual part of my recovery, requires work, as does every other relationship in my life. I need to hang out with God, as I hang out with other friends. I share with God my fears and troubles, my good news and accomplishments; then I'm still and listen for his reply.

In the morning, I read my OA and AA meditation books. I read Step Eleven from the AA "Twelve and Twelve" and Step Three from OA's "Twelve and Twelve." I thank God for another day to be abstinent and do his will. In the evening, I try to read some program literature: two pages from the Big Book or a story from *Abstinence* or the Brown Book (*Overeaters Anonymous*). I thank God for another day of abstinence and another day free from the food and body obsession.

What's most miraculous about this is that I do not consider it work. These actions are both part of my life and the very reason I have a life. As we say at the end of meetings, "Keep coming back. It works when you work it, and you're worth it!"

— *Texas USA*

# That's Spirituality!

Turning over to God the first disappointment of the day is spiritual. Walking to a store to buy abstinent food is spiritual. Walking farther to save ten or fifteen cents is spiritual. Straightening up the apartment is spiritual. Accomplishing what I set out to do is spiritual. Turning a problem over to my Higher Power is spiritual.

*Writing these thoughts and sending them to Lifeline is spiritual.*

Watching a children's TV show with a little neighbor is spiritual. Writing these thoughts and sending them to *Lifeline* is spiritual. Completing a daily OA reading is spiritual. Jotting down the most meaningful line from the reading so it's etched in my memory is spiritual, too.

Striving for abstinence and achieving it one day at a time is spiritual. Waiting for an OA friend to call or visit is spiritual. Sharing abstinent food and abstinent thoughts over coffee is spiritual. Taking a bath, washing my hair, putting lotion on my body, polishing my nails, and showing up at a meeting are spiritual.

Going to a movie in a new theater is spiritual. Staying abstinent with all the tempting goodies sold there is the utmost in spirituality. Singing, dancing, and whistling for joy are spiritual. Enjoying the simple things in life is another miracle of spirituality.

Spirituality is a newcomer reaching out to me because she hears the strength in my voice. Spirituality is really listening when a child speaks to me because sometimes God has a child's face. Receiving *Lifeline* in the mail today and devouring it from cover to cover instead of a food item I once coveted—that's spirituality.

— *Nevada USA*

# My God Box

Does your mind sometimes wander when you kneel to pray? Mine does. Why not write out your prayers and present them to God via a God Box?

Any box can be turned into a God Box. I used a box that diapers came in. I taped the top closed, and then cut a four-by-one-inch slot in the side. I wrote "God Box" on it with a felt-tip pen.

Sometimes I write out all the details of an event or situation. At other times, I write just a couple of words or someone's name, or I draw a picture on a small square of paper. I drop my prayers into the slot and give a sigh of relief that my request or frustration is now in God's hands.

Why not try it? You might be amazed with the results.

— *California USA*

# Holy Moments

"That feeling of uselessness and self-pity will disappear" (*Alcoholics Anonymous*, 4th ed., p. 84).

A couple of months ago, I woke up on a Saturday morning feeling different: lighter and more open-minded. I pondered on the feeling and realized that I had been waking up like this for many months, but the change had been so gradual I hadn't noticed the lessening of my mental burden.

It wasn't that way three years ago. Then I woke up every day knowing I was already a failure and would probably fail again. I knew the day would hold no wonder for me. I did that to myself. All day I worried about food.

I compared the two feelings and realized for the first time how far I have come in this program. I have had physical recovery and have maintained my body size for more than two years. I am wearing the same clothes this year that I wore last year and the year before. Is it a miracle? Yes, because I have never been able to do that. Is it the most miraculous thing that has happened to me? No.

The most miraculous thing is the burden my mind has lost: the burden of judging myself and others. The desire to judge still pops up and probably always will, but my Higher Power's will does not allow me to follow through on it. What a lesson learned and a load removed.

*Even if all I notice are the bubbles in my mop bucket, that's how I make every minute holy.*

I have lost the capacity to inhibit myself from experiencing the moment. I used to be caught up in tomorrow or yesterday, focusing on future possibilities or past pitfalls. Now I attend to reality, which is what I have right here, right now. Even if all I notice are the bubbles in my mop bucket, that's how I make every minute holy.

The feelings of uselessness and self-pity have not disappeared forever. They are lurking in my recovering psyche, ready to pounce if I give them a chance. Sometimes that happens, and when it does, it's time to do more work on myself and for myself.

I have to be as rigorously honest about my emotional health as I have been about my physical health. Sometimes I get sloppy, and a loosening tape measure tells me so. Instead of getting caught up in denial, I honestly evaluate my food plan. When I trust my Higher Power and am honest with myself, the tape measure tightens.

The same is true of my emotions. This is the area where my most honest work is done because if it's not done, then I lose my physical recovery as well.

Anger is my underlying theme whenever I get depressed and

start a downward spiral. I am basically a proud person, and it's a false pride based on an overloaded sense of entitlement. I have been good, so I deserve no less than whatever I desire. I have come to expect my Higher Power to deliver, and when he doesn't, I feel angry, hurt, rejected, depressed, and unholy. By analyzing my anger through an anger workbook, I've learned to be assertive with my Higher Power instead of whining and waiting for him to do all the work.

By working with my sponsor, I've learned to experience my deepest, darkest, saddest sense of self. Those emotions that I tried to stuff with food now have days or even weeks to work themselves out and become fully experienced. It helps me to draw word pictures about these feelings and describe them to God assertively.

My sponsor also helped me develop a series of affirmations that I use to pick myself up when I'm healing from the emotional colds I get:

∾ I radiate beauty.

∾ I am strong and courageous, and God is in control.

∾ I am patient and persistent, and life is good to me.

∾ I play an important role in the universe, and so do you!

∾ I am learning to forgive.

∾ I am a humble servant of the Lord.

That last one, along with others, has helped me with my inflated ego and false pride. It has dissolved the anger that flares up when I think I've been slighted. When I say it to myself, I immediately feel a sense of relief, clarity, and complete submission to the will of my Higher Power. It puts my life in perspective and my mind at ease, and it diverts the feelings of uselessness and self-pity that can destroy my sanity … if I allow it.

— *Arizona USA*

# A Gardener's Tale

I was on my hands and knees in the garden of my beach house. The radishes needed thinning, and the beans and eggplants had been devoured by a horde of compulsively overeating caterpillars. The only thing flourishing was the lush carpet of grass and weeds around the leafless stems of my crop.

In the next yard I could hear the hum of an electric hedge trimmer and a voice complaining that the hedge's height and width made it impossible for him to trim the far edge of the bushes. Figuring I could help out, I called over that he could trim from my side of the hedge.

When the gardener came into my yard, I asked if he would trim back the wild growth on my side of the hedge too. He readily agreed, and I went back to my weeding. I was flabbergasted when, after squaring off the top, he threw the trimmer back into my neighbor's yard and explained that he was out of time and would do my side when next he came—in about two months.

My blood boiled as I stalked off to the garage for a rake to clean up the trimmings he'd left in my yard. I muttered to myself as I hand-picked the leaves and twigs out of my sugarsnap peas. Grumbles spewed out of my mouth. But suddenly I found a pair of sunglasses stuck in the bushes. I realized they must belong to the gardener. As I threw them into the trash with the bush clippings, I thanked my Higher Power for this perfect opportunity to get revenge on the lying bushwhacker.

*I thanked my Higher Power for this perfect opportunity to get revenge on the lying bushwhacker.*

Some of my friends thought the story was hysterical. The jerk had gotten what he deserved. But my sponsor was shocked. I had the distinct impression that she had expected a different end to my story, but what other ending could it have? The creep had lied to me and left me with his mess!

Receiving no validation from my sponsor, I looked for it at my OA Twelve-Step study meeting. I was irked to receive the same reception. I paid no attention to the members sharing at the meeting, too busy listening to the voice in my own head: "After all, *he's* the one who lied. Back in the city we always have our gardener trim both our side and the neighbor's ..."

But suddenly I heard what was being said. A member was talking about the Twelfth Step as "practicing these principles in all our affairs." She said she'd never really grasped this part of the Step until someone at this very meeting had explained to her that it meant "rigorous honesty and choosing character building over comfort" in all our dealings. She continued: "So, when the cashier gives this person change for a twenty and she paid with a ten, she doesn't run out of the store chortling over her good fortune. She says, 'You've given me too much change.'"

I could feel my color rising as I listened. "To this person, abstinence is not just a way of eating, it's a way of life. That's what practicing these principles in all our affairs means to her."

My friend practiced the strictest anonymity: only she and I knew that the person she was talking about was me.

Her praises made me think about my encounter with the bushwhacker. "My resentment was justified," I thought. But I remembered what the Big Book says about resentment and self-righteous anger: "A life which includes deep resentment leads only to futility and unhappiness ... For when harboring such feelings we shut ourselves off from the sunlight of the Spirit" (*Alcoholics Anonymous*, 4th ed., p. 66). I asked myself: "Since when does your Higher Power give you opportunities for revenge? Your God is one of love, compassion, and kindness, not punishment and retribution. That was the God you gave away when you came to OA."

If this wasn't an opportunity for revenge, what was it? In an instant I knew the answer: an opportunity for *spiritual growth.*

I also realized that I had invited the gardener into my yard in the hope that he'd trim my side, too. Part of my anger came from not getting what I wanted. And I had told my story because I was looking for counsel. My innermost self had sought the program, the tools, and the Steps to put me back on track.

I grumbled all the way home. I cursed as I dug through the dirt, the clippings, and the caterpillar-chewed plant stems in the trash barrel. Of course, the glasses had slid all the way to the bottom of the barrel. I fished them out, wiped them off, brought them to my neighbor's house and told her what had happened.

"Thank you," she said, closing the door with no apology or even a promise to talk to the gardener. I laughed at my Higher Power's sense of humor. I didn't return the glasses for an apology. I did it for me: my recovery and my abstinence.

I got on my hands and knees again—to pull the weeds I had missed and to thank HP for giving me another chance to grow spiritually.

— *California USA*

1. We admitted we were powerless over food—that our lives had become unmanageable.

2. Came to believe that a Power greater than ourselves could restore us to sanity.

3. Made a decision to turn our will and our lives over to the care of God *as we understood Him.*

4. Made a searching and fearless moral inventory of ourselves.

5. Admitted to God, to ourselves, and to another human being the exact nature of our wrongs.

6. Were entirely ready to have God remove all these defects of character.

7. Humbly asked Him to remove our shortcomings.

8. Made a list of all persons we had harmed and became willing to make amends to them all.

9. Made direct amends to such people wherever possible, except when to do so would injure them or others.

10. Continued to take personal inventory and when we were wrong, promptly admitted it.

11. Sought through prayer and meditation to improve our conscious contact with God *as we understood Him,* praying only for knowledge of His will for us and the power to carry that out.

12. Having had a spiritual awakening as the result of these Steps, we tried to carry this message to compulsive overeaters and to practice these principles in all our affairs.

*Permission to use the Twelve Steps of Alcoholics Anonymous for adaptation granted by AA World Services, Inc.*

## THE TWELVE TRADITIONS OF OVEREATERS ANONYMOUS

1. Our common welfare should come first; personal recovery depends upon OA unity.

2. For our group purpose there is but one ultimate authority—a loving God as He may express Himself in our group conscience. Our leaders are but trusted servants; they do not govern.

3. The only requirement for OA membership is a desire to stop eating compulsively.

4. Each group should be autonomous except in matters affecting other groups or OA as a whole.

5. Each group has but one primary purpose—to carry its message to the compulsive overeater who still suffers.

6. An OA group ought never endorse, finance, or lend the OA name to any related facility or outside enterprise, lest problems of money, property, and prestige divert us from our primary purpose.

7. Every OA group ought to be fully self-supporting, declining outside contributions.

8. Overeaters Anonymous should remain forever nonprofessional, but our service centers may employ special workers.

9. OA, as such, ought never be organized; but we may create service boards or committees directly responsible to those they serve.

10. Overeaters Anonymous has no opinion on outside issues; hence the OA name ought never be drawn into public controversy.

11. Our public relations policy is based on attraction rather than promotion; we need always maintain personal anonymity at the level of press, radio, films, television, and other public media of communication.

12. Anonymity is the spiritual foundation of all these Traditions, ever reminding us to place principles before personalities.

*Permission to use the Twelve Traditions of Alcoholics Anonymous for adaptation granted by AA World Services, Inc.*